REFLECTIONS OF A LAWYER

REFLECTIONS OF A LAWYER

Second Edition

Keshav Dayal
Senior Advocate

Universal
Law Publishing Co.
NEW DELHI - INDIA

First Edition 2006
Second Edition 2011

ISBN : 978-81-7534-995-7

Published by
UNIVERSAL LAW PUBLISHING CO. PVT. LTD.
C-FF-1A, Dilkhush Industrial Estate,
(Near Azadpur Metro Station) G.T. Karnal Road,
Delhi-110 033
Tel : 011-27438103, 27215334, 42381334
Fax : 011-27458529
E-mail *(For sales inquiries)* : sales@unilawbooks.com
E-mail *(For editorial inquiries)* : edit@unilawbooks.com
Website : www.unilawbooks.com

Recommended citation: *Reflections of a Lawyer*, Keshav Dayal, 2nd Edn. (New Delhi: Universal Law Publishing Co. Pvt. Ltd., 2011)

Computer Typeset at Aesthetic & *Printed* at Mudrak, New Delhi.

Dedicated
to
my
Parents

हंस राज भारद्वाज
H.R. Bhardwaj

सत्यमेव जयते

मंत्री
विधि एवं न्याय
भारत सरकार
नई दिल्ली-110001
MINISTER
LAW & JUSTICE
GOVERNMENT OF INDIA
NEW DELHI-110001

September 27, 2005

FOREWORD

I am happy to know that Shri Keshav Dayal has completed 50 years in the profession as a practicing lawyer and 25 years as Senior Advocate and that his book "Reflections of a Lawyer" will be released on 24th October, 2005 to mark the occasion.

The struggle of a lawyer is similar to that of a warrior. His weapons of truth, hard work and sincerity contribute towards triumph. His invincible spirit and enthusiasm lay down examples for the common man to fight for justice. The contribution of Shri Keshav Dayal in diverse fields of law during his long professional career is well known.

I send my greetings on this occasion and wish Shri Keshav Dayal many more years of fruitful service to the community.

H.R. Bhardwaj

SAARC

S A A R C L A W

(South Asian Association for Regional Co-operation in Law)

Secretariat:
Kesar Dass House,
495, Udyog Vihar, Phase V,
NH-8, Gurgaon-122 016
National Capital Region
(Republic of India)
Tel: + 91-124-504 0193
Fax: + 91-124-504 0194
Email: info@saarclaw.com
Website: www.saarclaw.co

MESSAGE

I am indeed happy to convey this message on the occasion of the release of this meaningful and noteworthy publication by Mr. Keshav Dayal, Sr. Advocate, Supreme Court of India, who also happens to be Vice-President of SAARCLAW – India Chapter.

Mr. Keshav Dayal, is one of the most eminent and experienced lawyers today, known widely for his astute and pleasant demeanor. During his vast career as an Advocate, spanning five decades, he has not only acquired name as a skilled lawyer but has also made valuable contributions to the growth of legal profession as a whole. Being a member of various associations of lawyers and legal organizations, including, SAARCLAW – India Chapter, Indian Law Institute, Institute of Constitutional and Parliamentary Affairs, International Institute of Human Rights Society, he has actively promoted the growth of legal consciousness and profession.

This publication is another step of his to enrich legal literature and consciousness. I am glad that he has taken this step to compile his works of writing and am certain that all the readers shall stand to benefit from his wisdom. I wish him and this publication all the best and success.

Sd/-

HEMANT BATRA

Date: 5th of October, 2005

Secretary General SAARCLAW

THE BAR ASSOCIATION OF INDIA

Lalit Bhasin
Hony. General Secretary

Office:
10 Hailey Road,
10th Floor,
Dakshineshwar Building,
New Delhi-110 001
Phone: 23322601,
23326998
Fax: 2332 9273, 2335 7521
E-mail: lbhasin@vsnl.com

October 5, 2005

MESSAGE

Mr. Keshav Dayal, in my opinion, belongs to the Setalvad model of the profession-hardworking, clear headed and accurate presentation of facts and the law before the Court-without any twisting of facts or holding back judgements against his clients. He has been an impeccable, independent and fearless Officer of the Court in the true sense.

In addition to his heavy professional commitments, he has still managed to find time for affairs of the Bar-having held important positions. The Bar Association of India is privileged to have him as one of its distinguished and outstanding members.

We wish him many more decades of active professional life. On behalf of our President Mr. F.S. Nariman and the Governing Council we convey our Best Wishes & Greetings to Mr. Dayal on completion of 50 years in the profession.

Sd/-
LALIT BHASIN
Hony. General Secretary

Main Office: **The Bar Association of India**
93, Lawyers Chambers, Supreme Court of India, New Delhi
Phone : 23385902 • Fax : 23329273

PREFACE TO THE SECOND EDITION

The release of the first edition has been the source of great satisfaction to me. Not only was the book well received and commented by the Lawyers and Judges, but also by the press as well. The fact that the entire publication of the book in the first edition were all sold out, has not only given me immense satisfaction, but also provided the need for reprint of next edition. The messages which were received on the release of the book also shows that the book has won approval from the distinguished members of the Bar and Judiciary.

The congratulatory messages received on the release of the book include legal luminaries like Dr. Justice AR Lakshmanan, Former Judge, Supreme Court of India and Chairman, Law Commission, Mr. Justice Dalveer Bhandari, the then Chief Justice, Bombay High Court and now Judge of the Supreme Court, Mr. P. Chidambaram, Hon'ble Union Minister of Finance, Mr. Justice Y.V. Chandrachud, Former Chief Justice of India and Mr. Justice R.S. Pathak, Former Chief Justice of India, Mr. Justice Cyriac Joseph, Chief Justice of High Court of Uttaranchal, Late Dr. L.M. Singhvi, eminent Diplomat and Jurist and host of other important persons.

From the Press, the Hindu Newspaper came out and commented with the Heading "Standardization of fees will boost lawyers image" Similarly, The Tribune, Chandigarh, India-Nation also lauded the release of the said book. The Tribune commented on the book as under:—

> "In the book titled "Reflections of a Lawyer", released recently by Justice Sabharwal, the author has dealt with various important issues like image of a lawyer in the public mind, role of a legal professional, judicial activism, corruption in high places, transparency in appointment of judges, human rights, election laws, obscenity laws, law pertaining to arrest and preventive detention, mercy killing and delay in deciding cases in Indian courts." According to the Law Chronicle "The thoughts and ideas of the author are vividly shared through several mini-chapters which are quite interesting and amazing.

While all the articles are interesting articles like image of Lawyers in Public Mind, Supreme Court Bench direction in cases of Appearances in Person before the Supreme Court. Constitution of "Tribunals; Is consultation with Chief Justice of High Court necessary; are note worthy that give good deal of information to the users".

The poetries appearing at the end have been penned by me.

The book as pointed out in the preface of the first edition has been dedicated to my parents who have been the source of constant inspiration and guidance for me. Similarly, I am also indebted to the learned members of the profession and the superior members of the judiciary, who have appreciated the release of the book and I have hardly any words to extend my thanks for their kind gesture.

I am grateful to, my elder brother Mr. Prahlad Dayal, Advocate, who has helped in making necessary corrections and modifications in the 1st Edition. My Thanks are also due to Mr. Arun K. Beriwal, Advocate, who has helped in updating, the various judgments referred to in the articles appearing in the 1st publication, so that the Revised Edition contains references to the latest judgments of the Supreme Court, and would be beneficial to the lawyers, Judges and even the law students.

My thanks are also due to Sanjay Kumar Singh, Advocate, for topic research and for addition of the recent judgments upto July 2010 passed by the Hon'ble Supreme Court of India and including them in the revised edition of the book. References from the Year Book "Human Rights" 2008 & 2009, published by International Institute of Human Rights Society (Regd.) have also been included in the present revised edition of the book.

KESHAV DAYAL

February 2011 Senior Advocate and Author

VIEWS & REVIEWS

National Standardisation of fees will boost Lawyers image

The legal profession has its stalwarts who adhere to the' values of honesty, Impartially and upholding the principles of justice but that is not the image of the Bar as a whole. Values seem to be eroding and this has affected the functioning of organized groups like bar councils, says a new book.

One reason for the present day state of affairs Is the Influx of a large number of entrants to the profession without a proper legal education and background, but placing of restriction on new entrants is frowned upon, says the book 'Reflections of a Lawyer' by senior advocate Keshav Dayal.

The author who has completed his 50 years as a lawyer is Vice Chairman of SAARC Law and Vice-President of International Institute of Human Rights Society.

While raising questions like what is the Image of lawyers in public mind? Is the image of a professional people dedicated to the task of building an Indian society based on social, political and economic justice or is the•image that of a business person, out to make huge profits working on commercial lines, defending the rich, the elite and the chosen few, and working on the principles of expediency rather than justice?, the book says that the questions are not easy to answer.

The image of the lawyers would get a boost If some efforts are made to have standardization in respect of payment of fees to the lawyers and greater role by the Bar Council and Bar Associations to eradicate delays in delivery of justice, the book says. The book is a compilation of articles published in newspapers by the author.

Published in "the Hindu News Update Service" Sunday November 13, 2005

CJI, Law Minister laud Dayal's book on legal issues

Several noted jurists, including Chief Justice of India Y.K. Sabharwal and Law Minister H.R. Bhardwaj, have lauded the efforts of Senior Advocate Keshav Dayal to bring a book dealing with various legal aspects.

Among others who appreciated the efforts of Mr. Dayal, Vice-Chairman of SAARC Law India Chapter and associated with various other National and International Legal Organisations are, Finance Minister Mr. P. Chidambaram, Former Chief Justice of India Mr. Y.V. Chandrachud, Supreme Court of India Judge Mr. Delveer Bhandari, SAARC India Chapter, President and Former Apex Court Judge Mr. U.C. Banerjee, Supreme Court Bar Association President Mr. P.H. Parekh and Senior Advocate Mr. L.M. Singhvi.

In the book titled "Reflections of a Lawyer", released recently by Justice Sabharwal, the author has dealt with various Important issues like image of a lawyer in the public mind, role of a legal professional, judicial activism, corruption in high places, transparency in appointment of judges, human rights, election laws, obscenity laws, law pertaining to arrest and preventive detention, mercy killing and delay in deciding cases in Indian courts.

The book also contains poems written by Mr. Dayal, which had come for a special praise from Justice Chandrachud, who described the combination of an advocate and poet a "rare" thing to happen.

Describing the book as highly informative on legal issues, Justice Chandrachud said it made an excellent reading and would be of great help to young lawyers.

Seventy-two-year-old Dayal said he thought it appropriate to bring out a book on his experience in the profession and as a social worker on his completing 50 years in the profession.

The Tribune "Tribune News Service" New Delhi, November 3

Standardisation of fees will boost lawyers image

New Delhi, Nov. 13: The legal profession has its stalwarts who adhere to the values of honesty, impartiality and upholding the principles of justice but that is not the image of the Bar as a whole. Values seem to be eroding and this has affected the functioning of organized groups like bar councils, says a new book.

One reason for the present day state of affairs is the influx of a large number of entrants to the profession without a proper legal education and background, but placing of restriction on new entrants is frowned upon, says the book 'Reflections of a Lawyer' by senior advocate Keshav Dayal. The author who has completed his 50 years as a lawyer is Vice Chairman of SAARC Law and Vice President of International Institutes of Human Rights Society.

While raising questions like what is the image of lawyers in public mind? Is the image of a professional people dedicated to the task of building an Indian Society based on social, political and economic justice or is the image that of a business person, out to make huge profits working on commercial lines, defending the rich, the elite and the chosen few, and working on the principles of expediency rather than justice?, the book says that the questions are not easy to answer.

The image of the lawyers would get a boost if some efforts are made to have standardization in respect of payment of fees to the lawyers and greater role by the Bar Council and Bar Associations to eradicate delays in delivery of justice, the book says. The book is a compilation of articles published in newspapers by the author.

Judicial activism, which has been necessitated on account of failure of the executive and the legislature to live up to the high standards that are required and expected of them will continue to play an important role in the affairs of the nation, the author says.

Judicial activism by the Indian judiciary is not a recent phenomenon and the courts have been exercising their powers which could be termed as an exercise in judicial activism. Traces of judicial activism can be found even in earlier judgments, the book says.

On the criteria for selection and transparency in appointment of judges the author says that it is only when competent and independent persons are appointed to the judiciary that the independence of the judiciary can be guaranteed. The process of selection of judges should be such that it should inspire confidence in the people. It is therefore, of the utmost importance that great care should be taken in selection of judges, more so in the case of higher judicial appointments, he says.

Dayal, who is also an executive member of the International Institute of Human Rights Society says that the Supreme Court is the pioneer in defending human rights and has acted not only as protector but also implemented the human rights guaranteed by the Universal Declaration of Human Rights under Magna Carta.

Terrorism which through its recent strikes has shaken not only the Indian society but the entire world is a debatable issue the book says but cautions that if human rights are violated in the process of combating terrorism, it will be self defeating. Terrorism often thrives where human rights are violated, which adds to the need to strengthen action to combat violation of human rights".

He says that delay in the conclusion of cases is becoming frequent and seems to be on the increase. Most of the land and immovable property cases take years for disposal in the normal course. It is not uncommon to find litigation being continued from father to son and even grandsons. One of the reasons for delay in disposal of cases is seeking of unnecessary adjournments by the litigants, the author says. (PTI)

Daily Exelsior, New Delhi, November 13

PREFACE TO THE FIRST EDITION

I have been pouring my thoughts and ideas into articles and poems for long now. It is perhaps a deeply embedded desire of mine to organize and communicate my thoughts. That was, I believe, the foremost reason for contributing to different magazines and newspapers. When thoughts surged I put them in articles and when it was strong emotions they came out in poetry. This book is a compilation of both my prose and poetry besides some of my published letters to the editors that appeared in different dailies. I regularly wrote for *Lawteller* and many of the articles included in this collection appeared therein.

I have dedicated this book to my parents who have been the source of constant inspiration and pillars of strength against which I could always lean in times of difficulty.

I am also deeply indebted to my wife, who has always been by my side through thick and thin and without whom life would not have been this smooth.

My son and daughter have always been the flowers that made me smile when I got back home from a hard day's work. Today my grandchildren have taken over the role of their parents to keep it light for me no matter how hard things get.

I am thankful to Mr. Hem Raj Singh, Legal Editor, Universal Law Publishing Co. Pvt. Ltd., for giving such a decent shape to the book.

I am also grateful to Mr. Manish Arora, Editorial Director, Universal Law Publishing Co. Pvt. Ltd., for his constant encouragement and unflinching support without which this book was not possible.

September, 2005 **KESHAV DAYAL**

CONTENTS

PART IV

LAW AND HUMAN RIGHTS

PART V

IN THE SPIRIT OF LETTERS

PART VI

POETICALLY YOURS

KESHAV DAYAL:
AN ADVOCATE AND A GENTLEMAN

*HemRaj Singh**

Life devices different ways to chisel people into the best they could be. Some people whine and cry, disgruntled and dissatisfied, while some just play along. Then, a few play along well. Keshav Dayal is one such fellow who did just that – and did it very well – despite his profession being not the one he dreamt of. Born (1933) and brought up in a prominent *Mathur Kayasth* family at old *Haveli Jugal Kishore* in Chandni Chowk, Old Delhi, Dayal was drawn to the forces, fascinated by the disciplined life of the men in uniform. He wanted to join Navy or Air Force, but his father, strongly disapproved it, almost tore his application forms. That was the end of his first career choice – or shall we say, it was the beginning of the career he was to distinguish himself in. His father, Mr. Bishamber Dayal, was a Senior Advocate with a roaring practice and wanted his son to join him, which Keshav Dayal finally did. And as they say, there was no looking back.

Keshav went to a government school, Ramjas Higher Secondary School, where his fee was Rs. 10, as he was considered to belong to a well off family. Of his school days he clearly remembers his principal, Mr. Datta, who was a strict disciplinarian, who did not allow any latitude to those who played well and studied less for that reason – an anti-sports pedagogue, in short. Another thing that he remembers of those days is Quit India Movement and freedom fighters' pitched battle against British Imperialism. He passed out from school with science subjects at the age of 16 to join St. Stephen's College for B.A. (Hons.) in Mathematics.

Having come from a school where one could indulge in sports only at one's own risk, he found a sports-favouring St. Stephen's very different. He joined Elocution Club and played Tennis and Cricket, but considers himself mediocre in both. Armed with a B.A. (Hons.) degree in Mathematics, he joined the Faculty of Law, Delhi University, in 1952. This time he did better at sports and other extracurricular activities and became Secretary of the Faculty of Law, Social Work Society and was also the Honorary Secretary (Tennis), Delhi University Athletic Association. He also represented his institution in Tennis and Table Tennis, and received a certificate of merit. He spent his spare time reading, and the book that left lasting impression on him, besides the teachings of Swami Vivekanand, was Mahatma Gandhi's *"The Story of My Experiments with Truth."*

* Editor, Universal Law Publishing Co. Pvt. Ltd., New Delhi.

Mr. Dayal entered the profession of law in 1955 joining his father, who had lots of work as a Central Government Counsel in Delhi High Court and as a Counsel for Income-tax and other government departments. He plunged into the profession headlong and started working with religious devotion. He cites an interesting incident when a client entered his office and showed papers of his tenancy asking for the advice as to from what time should he show himself to be the tenant in order to take the maximum benefit of the law. He asked the client to state truthfully as to since when he was the tenant. The client informed him that it was a part of a lawyer's job to turn black into white and *vice-versa*. The next thing he did was showing him the door. Leaving, the person had a declaration to make – that Mr. Dayal could never be a successful lawyer. The declaration rang hollow then, and rings hollower now. Falsehood, this man always detested.

Mr. Dayal became the Chief Legal Advisor of the DDA in 1967 at a relatively early age of 34 and continued for 11 long years as sole Chief Legal Advisor. He was designated as Senior Advocate and became the first Standing Counsel for the DDA and held office till 1982. There he headed the entire legal section of the Law Officers, Counsels and the staff. He appeared in a number of cases for DDA and some of the memorable ones have been those relating to prosecutions of landowners by the DDA for violating the Master Plans. In a number of writ petitions it was argued that the prosecutions should be quashed for want of the zonal plans. Mr. Dayal successfully argued for the DDA before a Full Bench of Delhi High Court. He also appeared for the DDA in a number of cases filed in the Delhi High Court challenging the acquisition of land by the DDA, and could convince the Court in DDA's favour. He has also been the Counsel for the MCD and the Food Corporation of India.

As a Senior Government Counsel he appeared for the Archaeological Survey of India in a number of cases relating to important historical monuments like Qutab Minar, Char Minar, etc. In Jama Masjid case pertaining to illegal encroachments he visited the monument pursuant to the Directives of the Court.

He also represented Border Security Force (B.S.F.) in a number of important cases where court martial proceedings were challenged on account of violations of BSF Act and the rules framed thereunder.

When he was appointed a Senior Advocate, not much prestige was attached to it and was, therefore, often ridiculed by his friends and colleagues on that account. Things are different now and his friends probably would no longer be that happy about the laughs they had. Mr. Dayal has been a Senior Advocate for 25 years now and has completed 50 years in practice.

A FAMILY MAN

Mr. Dayal married Roop, who comes from a well-known Mathur family in Agra, in 1959. Mr. Dayal frankly admits that without her active support he could not have achieved the success he enjoys today. But then things have not always been smooth on this front, and in a tragic accident a heavy tree branch fell on Mrs. Dayal, on account of which she sustained injuries to her spine and had to spend 6 torturous months under medical supervision. She also developed a brain tumour but has been, thankfully, cured of it at VIMHANS two years back. However, having taken all these jolts in her stride she is back to a normal life except for the stick that she needs to help her walk.

Except for these hitches Mr. Dayal has had a very satisfactory family life and is blessed with a son, Deepak, and a daughter, Alka, who is happily married to Mr. Sanjay Prasad, Manager, New India Insurance Company. Sanjay comes from a family of lawyers. His father was a lawyer and grandfather, Justice Girish Prasad, a judge of Allahabad High Court. Deepak and his wife Nutan have a daughter, Mrinalini (16) and a son, Himanshu (12) while Alka has a son, Ashish, who is now an Engineer working with Tata Consultancy Services and a daughter, Aditi, who is in her Final year of Engineering. Mr. Dayal, thus, has quite a bubbly household with four grandchildren.

A SOCIAL MAN

Mr. Dayal, besides being a noted lawyer and a family man, has also been a man of society and has associated with United Lawyers Association, as its Vice-President, has been Vice-President, SAARC LAW-India Chapter and is with International Human Rights as Executive Member. He has also been the Vice-President, Delhi High Court Bar Association and has had the privilege of having Mr. Y.K. Sabharwal (former Chief Justice of India) as Honorary Secretary and Mr. B.N. Kirpal (former Chief Justice of India) as Treasurer during his tenure.

He was not just an active member of the legal fraternity but also associated with the world outside legal circle. He has been the President, Lions Club, Central Delhi/Delhi, South and has been awarded a certificate of merit by the Club for his 25-year-long association with it. He did not leave sports either and was Vice-President, Delhi Lawn Tennis Association for a number of years.

Mr. Dayal has been a man of different hues and has led a fulfilling life with all his social duties well performed and causes aptly served. He has been an obedient son, a loving husband and father, a doting grandfather, a responsible member of the society, and of course an able lawyer. What more can one ask of a man.

DAYAL THOUGHTS: *AN INSIGHT INTO THE MAN AND HIS BELIEFS*

*HemRaj Singh**

When I dialled Mr. Keshav Dayal's number the first time, I expected to hear a rather firm voice with a business-like tone to it. A lawyer of long standing is quite a hardened professional, often. I did not have any special reason to expect it of Mr. Dayal, and perhaps would not even have taken note of this sub-conscious assumption, had Mr. Dayal not shattered it so completely. The voice was crystal clear, the tone polite and respectful and the words measured, well chosen and spoken very delicately. And then I worked with him on the first edition of this book, but the true revelation came when we started with the second edition, as it was then that he handed over to me a bunch of papers gone yellow from aging. That was his collection of random thoughts jotted down and preserved since 1952. They are demonstrative of Mr. Dayal's ability to think about things other than those that the law is concerned with. It is certainly very heartening to note that a busy lawyer found time to think about the world around and also thought of ways to improve it. So long as a responsible citizen is thinking of improving his surroundings and the lives that go on alongside – and around – his own, the hope remains alive. Most of us are just too busy living our own lives to think of anything else. Therefore, I decided to have this book enriched by a few selected thoughts of Mr. Dayal.

Struggles are normally seen as obstacles, which, to some extent, they are. What we overlook is that in them lies a – rare/exceptional incomparable teacher. Here is what Mr. Dayal says about it:

> *Struggles should not be averted, they should be faced squarely – nay, it should be welcomed otherwise what would life be worth without a struggle.*

After all there is no fun going on living without having a hurdle to overcome. The sense of achievement lies in realizing that one could swim against the current. Thus goes Mr. Dayal:

> *If you are not failing and struggling in this life, well, something is wrong somewhere, for failing is as much part of life as success.*

Very well said. Success doesn't teach as much as failure does, after all.

> *Success will be meaningless without the idea of failure. What matters in life is not that you won or lost but that you struggled.*

Now, this thought might appear be to a little too spiritual, but, in fact it is the essence of noble life.

---

* Editor, Universal Law Publishing Co. Pvt. Ltd., New Delhi.

> *The way to achieve anything in the life is to renounce it. Renunciation is the best mode of achievement in life. Renunciation means active and constant work without the idea of any reward.*

Sounds self-contradictory? It might 'sound' that way but there is no contradiction here because the pleasure that comes with achieving something does not come from the thing or object achieved but from the sense of having achieved something. And with it also comes the fear of losing the thing or object achieved and the desire to preserve and protect it. This is the source of unhappiness. Therefore, achieving without attaching much importance to what is achieved is the key to lasting happiness. This is what Mr. Dayal is pointing out when he talks of working relentlessly without thinking of the results and rewards.

In the idea of detached or selfless work above, religious undertones are unmistakable. The same is also evident here:

> *If you have given up all your life for the service of humanity, or society, do not think high of yourself. Thank God, for having the privilege to be an instrument of God for the good of the humanity.*

> This reminds me of John Milton's *On His Blindness*, wherein the poet concludes, *"They also serve who only stand and wait."*

The idea of selfless service also appeals Mr. Dayal quite a lot. He says:

> *Service should not form part of your life, on the contrary your whole life should centre round the basic idea of service...Do not be proud of your unselfish service, for has not service raised your soul to a stand and which would have been unattainable without it.*

However, selfless service does appeal to Mr. Dayal but he does not look down upon selfishness either. Now, here is a slight departure from the religious-spiritual stream of thought, and Mr. Dayal seems to shift close to Ayn Rand's idea of selfish pursuance of one's own happiness, regarding one's own happiness above everything else. He says:

> *Attainment of true happiness is a sacred aim and should not be looked down upon. Benefit of society in all its aspects as should be our ideal rather than the dim idea of self-realization, for it does not seem to concern itself with this world.*

Mr. Dayal regards the idea of self-realization as 'dim', apparently for the reason that it is, to his mind, more conceptual than real. Happiness, on the other hand, is far more tangible than an idea of 'self-realization', which might be rather illusionary. Pursuit of happiness, therefore, is a worthy goal. Being a man of reason, Mr. Dayal does not seem to believe too strongly in the unseen and unverifiable.

Life cannot be lived purposelessly and selfish pursuit of happiness with utter disregard of everything else might lead to sorrow. Mr Dayal, therefore, attaches life and living with higher principles and ideals, and says thus:

> *If you have some principles and ideals which you hold sacred you will have something to live for and realize in your life* i.e., *you will live for a purpose. Your sincere love, joy and the sacrifice that you joyfully undergo in holding these principles shall give you permanent and everlasting faith in permanent and eternal values* i.e., *faith in God. Your life will be a source of inspiration and guidance to others. If at certain time or times you fail to hold your principles due to whatever circumstances, you will feel miserable and uneasy, your conscience will prick you. In such circumstances you should pray to God to give you strength enough to follow the principles. Your prayers will be answered. You will then work with increased faith in your principles. Your principles will give you more powers than you can dream of. You will also cultivate self-control thereby. Self-control automatically follows from adherence to the principles, for you will have to undergo many hardships to uphold your principles, and you would learn to control yourself in the process.*

Here Mr. Dayal is conscious of the failures that might lie in one's way while pursuing higher ideals and principles. He is conscious of the fact that it is not possible to uphold and live by one's principles in all circumstance, and no matter how hard one tries there are bound to be failures. On such occasions he advises one to take recourse to prayers. Faith comes in handy in such cases. Talking of faith and religion, he says:

> *Religion teaches us non-attachment. When one is perfectly non-attached to worldly things* i.e. *is perfectly un-selfish, one thinks of helping others thereby raising his soul to a higher level. The work thus done for the benefit of the country shall be called social work. Will this be called probably too much of religious idealism?*

Mr. Dayal starts with the doctrine of *nishkam karmayoga* (dispassionate discharge of duties) and gives it a pragmatic shape chiseling out the spiritual aspect of the teaching and talking only of the practical use it can be put to. He fleetingly talks about 'raising' one's 'soul' and quickly moves to its social and national usefulness. Towards the end he also dismisses it as 'too much of religious idealism'. He doesn't seem to have much faith in human understanding of spiritual matters. Therefore, while he does understand its relevance but when it comes to communicating, he only puts across its socially relevant aspects. Since this is a younger Keshav Dayal writing around 1970 or so, it is possible that he himself wasn't all that sure about the spiritual dimensions of religion but was very much aware of its social face. So, he presented what he was sure of and kept to himself what he was just beginning to understand. One of the most debated religious ideas is 'vanity', and Mr. Dayal firmly believes in shunning it as best as one could. He cites Gandhiji thus:

> *Throw out the idea of vanity and self from you. Introspect each and every act of yours and reflect all those, or as many as possible acts which are selfish and increase all those that are un-selfish. Let this be the guiding principle. Let all your acts be dedicated to God. Then the idea of self and of reward will automatically vanish. Manliness consists in doing the right thing and facing the consequences of it boldly.*

Mr. Dayal once again advocates the path of selfless action here. He by quoting Gandhiji has supported the idea of not seeing one as the actor but dedicating all that one does to the Supreme Being, thereby completely dropping vanity from one's personality. This is also what Lord Krishna says in *Shrimad Bhagwad Gita*. Mr. Dayal sees religion as an inexhaustible source of inspiration. He writes:

Religion is an inexhaustible fountain of inspiration. It inspires you to do great things by following the right path. So let religion guide you in every place and every time, and all your actions.

Another religious tenet that Mr. Dayal firmly believes in is 'tolerance'.

> *Self-control teaches you tolerance. When you control your feelings; actions and thoughts you come to know of the various difficulties. You fail many times but go on succeeding if you are very sincere. When you yourself have failed time and again, you must realise how difficult it is for other persons to perform well and should not judge him harshly. You shall then not be angry with him but tolerate him and his views. You shall then not hate him, but love him (not for the sake that he has a soul which is divine and that he has to realize himself only, but as a man who has limitations, who is human, who is arrogant, etc.) the limitations can be of body, mind and circumstances, heredity, nature of man, etc. and it is no joke for anyone to break through these and therefore you will love and understand all persons better for you know how difficult this path is.*

This, in a way, is the fundamental principle enshrined in all religions without exception. And Mr. Dayal realizes and feels very strongly for it. In order to inculcate tolerance one needs self-restraint. Controlling one's mind and body is from where all things good start. Mr. Dayal says in this regard:

While controlling your body and mind, you will invariably ask what is to be done at the present? You will understand that what you were doing, was not very good for there is nothing such as absolute wrong. Some things are good and the rest are better, that's all. As soon as you start thinking in terms of un-selfishness the whole vision of the whole world will change. Do not worry then.

Think boldly, increase your ability, and start working for the benefit of the country and other good works. Only three things are desirable. First is self-control, second is faith and third is courage. These are the three essentials and should be cultivated first.

Despite advocating religious tenets Mr. Dayal is no blind follower of religion. He does not shirk from putting religion under the scanner. This is what he says about 'true religion':

True religion does not depend and should not depend upon the following:

(1) *How you dress, or what dress you wear every time and at times.*

(2) *How you eat or what you eat every time and at times.*

(3) *Whether you lead a rich man's life or a poor man's life.*

(4) *If you play a game, how you play or what you play.*

(5) *Customs of a place or caste rules and laws. They may depend upon social status or environments.*

It is only desirable that for religious advancements, you should lead a selfless unattached and plain life. You may start with any thing whatsoever, the rest shall follow easily. One step towards religion makes you a different man. We do not need rishis who sit in the Himalayas for self-realization and do not give the benefit of their spiritual life to humanity. Selfless social workers and real patriots can be the product of religion only.

Mr. Dayal, therefore, detaches religion from local customs, and associates it with leading a pure life free of all worldly attachments. His religion, therefore, lies in leading a simple, untangled life. He, in fact, looks down upon those sages who selfishly pursue self-realization because the society does not get benefited from their work. To Mr. Dayal a religious person is the one who selflessly works for the benefit of others. The *karmayoga* part of religion seems to appeal to Mr. Dayal more than any other aspect of religion. His view of religion is essentially utilitarian. This is evident from what he writes here:

We judge a thing by its utility (utility here means benefit to the society). It is a good standard to judge things but in many cases the utility or its value is not apparent on its face, for example a mathematician is sitting and working out new problems, thinking out new things. Ask him whether it is doing any good to any body. Invariably the answer will be in negative. After some time it may be discovered that the results that were thought out by the mathematician have been of immense benefit to the society. In this case utility is seen later on. So is the case with the works of poets, philosophers and even scientists. Some things may not have utility in the present set up, so does that mean that they should be rejected as no good. A duty may not always seem beneficial to others, nevertheless it is to be followed. In religion, the Karma part is the part which benefits the society as such i.e., *can be judged from the utility aspect. The Jyana part, and the Bhakti part do not have much utility on the face of them, but they are ultimately conducive to good. What is right or wrong action, which is the right duty, etc. will be decided with the help of Jyana, which help us to develop the intellect and only then the act is to be done. If we are tremendously active, but our works are not good, the result will be chaotic. Bhakti essentially deals with love, humility and generosity. This is also essential for Karma to be beneficial to the society. However, in certain high religious principles, the utility cannot be easily seen as in renunciation, unattachment and sacrifice, and Brahmcharya, etc. It is idle to see any utility in moksha, which is one of the highest aims of religion. In most religious matters however utility is easily seen. On the whole the test or utility may be applied to religious as well as spiritual matters. I am sure this will only help the cause of religion and will make it active, dynamic and more beneficial for all.*

Mr. Dayal, therefore, regards religion as something that has to be judged inside out before being followed. Every principle, religious or otherwise, has to be judged on the touchstone of general utility to human beings at large before being adhered to. Mr. Dayal, however, is conscious that there can be a few things whose benefit might not be apparent right away but might prove to be beneficial in the long run. He is a strong believer in the doctrine of selfless action and praises Pandit Nehru for his Karma centered approach to life.

Pandit Nehru's approach towards life is a dynamic approach having a touch of idealism and realism with it. It is a bold man's approach. Pandit Nehru has faith and character, has cultivated and developed fine moral qualities in him (Yet he does not claim to be religious) and finally he has firm faith in India's glory. He has the necessary courage and will and works earnestly and incessantly for the fulfilment of these ideals. One cannot but be impressed by the life and lofty ideals of Pandit Nehru.

Talking of Pandit Nehru and Gandhiji and their respective social perception, Mr. Dayal says:

Pandit Nehru believes in hard and sincere work. He believes in physical and mental development of the whole society. He dislikes the idea of suffering for the sake of suffering immensely. Enjoyment, happiness, work, decent life have their correct place in Nehruism. The idea of self-negation and sacrifice is also disliked by Panditji. He believes in a system that would not produce poor people. He immensely hates poverty and illiteracy. He disagrees with Gandhiji who seems to idolize poverty by saying that God is for the poor (Daridra Narayana). Both fight poverty, illiteracy and social

> *evils, but with different mental approach. Plain living does not cut much ice with Nehruism. Pandit Nehru is a real* Karma Yogi *and has in my opinion stressed the Karma side of religion.*

From his thoughts, ideals and idols, Mr. Dayal comes across as someone very conscious about life and the art of living. He is a person who believes in living a life based on sound principles, but before subscribing to a principle he puts it to a thorough lawyer-like scrutiny. He is not a blind follower but a cautious student of life.

MY BRIEF ENCOUNTERS WITH THE HIGH AND MIGHTY

I am reminded of my meetings with some of the historical personalities in interesting circumstances, which I am narrating below:—

(1) **Meeting with Pandit Jawaharlal Nehru.**—During the disturbances in 1947, during summer vacations we had left our residence and gone to Mussouri for a short stay. The building where we were staying was very close to a building called *'Baharestan'*. I used to go for a walk and while going on my walk in the morning, I saw the former Prime Minister Pandit Jawaharlal Nehru riding a horse and he came close by. During those days in 1947, the way of greeting was *'Jaihind'*. However, on account of sheer surprise, I greeted him with *'Adabarz'*, which is generally used in our household where Urdu was spoken. Surprisingly, he also responded with a very hearty return of *Adabarz*. I cherish this moment of my greeting our former Prime Minister till now. I read his book "Discovery of India" subsequently, and have been greatly influenced by his philosophy, and thoughts, which can be a guiding inspiration to the Indian people.

(2) **Meeting with Smt. Indira Gandhi.**—Some of our lawyer friends were called by Smt. Indira Gandhi at her residence in the morning. We received a message through a colleague. We reached her house at the appointed time and were all sitting in a room. We were all introduced, and I had been introduced as Chief Legal Adviser, DDA. On my introduction she responded by saying that the DDA should think more about the common man and they should devise substitute for the bricks for construction of houses, which were costlier. She suggested that some other substitute should be thought of which will make the houses cheaper and viable for the poor people. Of course as Chief Legal Adviser, I had hardly any role in this matter, but I still relish this meeting which shows a great love of the former Prime Minister, Smt. Indira Gandhi towards common men.

(3) **Meeting with A.D. Pandit, Chief Commissioner of Delhi.**—My father was a strict disciplinarian and would not introduce his sons to any VIP or seek anybody's help in promoting his sons. My father had to go and meet the Chief Commissioner and the driver did not come in time and I accompanied my father as driver to the residence of the Chief Commissioner. My father asked me to stay outside and went inside to meet the Chief Commissioner. When they came out I stood up and told the Chief Commissioner that I was the son of Mr.

Bishamber Dayal, and was a practicing Advocate. He liked this spirit of mine very much and said that he was very happy to meet me.

(4) **Meeting with Lt. Governor Dr. Amarnath Jha.**—I was the Chief Legal Adviser of DDA and did not get an opportunity of personal meeting with the Lt. Governor of Delhi who was the Chairman of DDA. Dr. Amarnath Jha, was the Lt. Governor of Delhi. His brother was the Vice-Chancellor of the Banaras Hindu University. I felt that I should at least properly meet the Lt. Governor. Whenever I rang up his Private Secretary and asked for an interview he would give sometime in working days in the morning, which was quite unsuitable to me as I had a number of cases in the High Court to attend. I talked about this matter to Mr. S.G. Bosemullick, Vice-Chairman, DDA, and he promised to take me along with him to the next meeting of the DDA. Such meetings were arranged by the Secretary and not by the Private Secretary to the Lt. Governor.

I was personally introduced to the Lt. Governor, who asked me if I had any difficulty. I told him that it was very difficult for me to meet the Lt. Governor in the working days, as I was busy in the High Court. He laughed and said I was always most welcome to drop in at his residence on any Saturday in the morning without prior appointments. I also pointed out that I had not been allotted any residence by the DDA. He tried to get in touch with the Chief Secretary, in my presence. However, I could not avail of these offers but I really admired these gestures, which showed his concern for me.

(5) **Meeting with Kunwar Mahmood Ali Khan, former Governor, Madhya Pradesh.**

I had the opportunity of meeting, Kunwar Mahmood Ali Khan, former Governor of Madhya Pradesh. The opportunity came across in a different manner. I was recommended to take a young man in my chamber as a Junior. The boy was no other than the 2nd son of the former Governor Kunwar Mahmood Ali Khan named Shahid Ali Rao.

I got not only the opportunity of meeting him but also staying at the Raj Bhawan, when we (my wife and myself) were invited to Shahid Ali Rao's wedding.

It was a memorable experience staying with the Governor, and attending all the ceremonies of a Muslim family, in all traditional style.

I came to know all the members of his family, closely and at personal level. Kunwar Sahib was very secular and broadminded and a man of strong convictions, widely respected by the people of Bhopal. His 3rd son, Javed Mamood also worked with me in my chambers. Both the sons, Shahid and Javed are practicing lawyers and well established now.

These are small incidents but I remember them till these days, as they have left a lasting impression on my mind.

MY FIRST COURT APPEARANCES

My First Appearance in the Supreme Court

I vividly remember a case I appeared in before the Supreme Court long back. It was a Special Leave Petition (SLP) filed by the Food Corporation of India (FCI) in the Apex Court against the decision of the High Court dismissing the objections filed against the arbitration award. As it was my first case in the Supreme Court I thought it proper to sit in the Court right from the beginning to see how cases were argued, and the reactions of the Hon'ble Judge (Hon'ble Mr. Justice D.A. Desai).

Earlier, in the couple of cases taken up for hearing before my case was called the judge strongly denounced filing of the appeals by the public authorities against the arbitration awards. In the case earlier to mine the judge imposed a cost of Rs. 25,000 on the applicant. When my case was called, the judge made remarks as to who had advised filing of the appeal in the Supreme Court. Prompt was my reply "the appeal was not filed by me, it was filed at the advice of the Law Department of the Corporation". Of course, the SLP was dismissed without any further arguments. I was happy that at least my clients were not burdened with any special cost, as had been done in the earlier case.

My First Case before the High Court

I was practicing with my father, and in those days it was a Circuit Bench of Punjab High Court, functioning at Rajpur Road, Civil Lines, Delhi. A client came to me and told that he wanted to file an appeal against the order dismissing his transfer petition in a criminal case. I had absolutely no idea whether any petition could be filed in the High Court, and if so, under which section of the Criminal Procedure Code. Rai Bahadur Nanak Chand, a Senior Counsel was also sitting beside me. He asked me to accept the case for being filed in the High Court. I examined, thereafter, provisions of the Criminal Procedure Code and subsequently filed the petition. That was my first case in the High Court. I do not remember the outcome of the case.

My First Case before the Magistrate's Court

While practicing in the Circuit Bench of the Punjab High Court, a client contacted me for filing a case for quashing of the criminal proceedings pending against him under section 420 of IPC. My client was a Cloth Seller and the charge was that there was an element of cheating in his dealing with clients on selling the cloth at wholesale rates. I was told that the Magistrates do not hear the case and have hardly any time for listening to the rulings cited before them. I prepared the case thoroughly, and I was able to find a number of rulings for quashing of the charge, as the case was of a civil nature, and the prosecution's case was not sustainable.

I went to the Magistrate's court with a number of law books with me. To my great surprise he listened to all of my arguments with attention and permitted me to cite all the rulings from the law books which I had brought with me. Immediately after the arguments the judge pronounced the judgment quashing the criminal proceedings against my client. It was my solitary experience before the court of a Magistrate. I carry a fond memory of it.

Memorable Instances

I recall one interesting instance in a case conducted by me long back. I was practicing at the Circuit Bench of the Punjab High Court at Rajpur Road. The petition had to be filed which was coming up for hearing before Hon'ble Mr. Justice Tek Chand, the Learned Judge was reputed to be an expert of English and English literature. While drafting the writ petition the word Annexure was to be typed. I specifically looked up the chambers English Dictionary for getting the correct spelling of the word. I kept English Dictionary book with me on the date of hearing. When the case came up for hearing before his Lordship the first question was about the correct spelling of the word Annexure. Since I had the dictionary with me I was able to satisfy the learned judge that the spelling of the word was correct. Thereafter, there was no difficulty in getting the case admitted by his Lordship. It is, sometimes, nice to know about the special interests of a particular judge when arguing a case before him.

TABLE OF CASES

F

G

H

I

J

K

L

Part I
Law and Lawyers

LAW AND LAWYERS

IMAGE OF LAWYERS IN PUBLIC MIND*

Lawyers have played a prominent part, not only in the freedom struggle, but in earlier days also, in shaping Indian history. Names of eminent lawyers come to one's mind who were revolutionaries and pioneers in eradicating the social evils existing in the Indian society. March to Indian freedom was not one isolated instance and pioneering work that had been done in raising the Indian society from the deep mires in which it had been entrenched. The names of the galaxy of lawyers like Mahatma Gandhi, father of the Nation; Motilal Nehru, Bhulabhai Desai, Chaman Lal Setalvad and a host of others come into vision, at once. The freedom struggle and thereafter the independence ushered in a new era. With the enforcement of the Indian Constitution new horizons and visions of social, economic, and political justice had been enshrined, and the role of lawyers in framing of the Constitution cannot but be over-emphasised. Introduction of clause of equal justice and free legal aid by the 42nd Amendment Act, 1976, was again a Constitutional landmark for the role assigned to Lawyers.

However, the question is what is the image of lawyers in public mind. Is the image that of professional people dedicated to the task of building an Indian society based on justice social, political and economic, or is the image that of business persons, out to make huge profits, working on commercial lines, defenders of the rich, the elite and the chosen few, and working on principles of expediency rather than of justice? What is the present image of those lawyers appearing for the States, Union of India and public bodies in courts of law? Is the image that of independent, upright law officers doing the duty fearlessly and independently, for the social good?

The question is not easy to answer. There are still stalwarts in the profession, adhering to the values of honesty, impartiality and independence of the Bar and upholding the principles of justice but that is not the image of the Bar, as a whole. Values seem to be declining, as in some other fields. The erosion of values has also affected the

* A paper published by the Bar Association of India; 8-10 August, 1997, p. 125.

functioning of the organised group of lawyers, *viz.* the Bar Councils, Bar Associations and other representative bodies. Success cannot be taken for granted for honest and hard working lawyers and their allegiance to the powerful groups makes all the difference, in the professional status. One reason for the state of present day affairs is the influx of a very large number of entrants to the profession without a proper legal education, and background. Placing of restriction on the entrants to the profession by providing of higher educational standards and specialised courses, is being frowned upon.

A fresh law graduate accordingly is from the very first day of enrolment, entitled and deemed fit to practice, not only in the district court, but in the High Courts and even in the Supreme Court. Similarly a person on retirement from any field whatsoever, having obtained Law degree at any point of time, is deemed fit for admission to the legal profession.

The insistence seems to be that the profession of law is entirely open, and one should fend for himself in the open free forum. If law has to be a forum of social justice, the orientation in thinking has to be done. Legal education will require to be modified, if lawyers have to discharge the role of instrumentality of ushering in social justice, and playing their due role in public life.

Image of lawyers in the public mind, would also be effected by the role the lawyers play in respect of legal aid programmes to the needy and the indigent. Legal aid programme has been initiated in various States, and the response of the lawyers to the same would also determine their public image.

Another important aspect of the lawyers' image is the role which the Bar Council, Bar Association and other Lawyers groups, will play in eradicating the delay, and in delivering quick and prompt justice to the people. Unfortunately, no concrete efforts have been made by the lawyers in suggesting ways and means for quick disposal of cases and to ensure that a litigant gets quick and prompt relief from the law courts. Some efforts are being made in this direction but the same require stepping up. Concrete steps have to be evolved by the lawyers and in particular the Bar Councils who are charged with the statutory duties to come out with complete and comprehensive programmes in this direction.

Lastly, the image of lawyers would also get a further boost if some efforts are made to have a standardisation in respect of payment of fees to the lawyers. There is some standardisation available in the case of senior advocates who are paid daily fee for appearance in the courts. Evolution of some voluntary code in respect of payment of fees to the lawyers would also be a welcome step to boost the image of lawyers in the country. Regarding the role of Lawyers reference is made to the latest judgment of the Supreme Court of India in the case of *R.K. Anand* v. *Registrar of Delhi High Court*,[1] decided by a Bench of three judges. The role of the lawyers has been commented upon in the following manner:—

> "The other important issue thrown up by this case and that cause us both grave concern and dismay is the decline of ethical and professional standards among lawyers. The conduct of the two appellants (one convicted of committing criminal contempt of court and the other found guilty of misconduct as Special Public Prosecutor), both of them lawyers of long standing, and designated Senior Advocates, should not be seen in isolation. The bitter truth is that the facts of the case are manifestation of the general erosion of the professional values among lawyers at all levels. We find today lawyers indulging in practices that would have appalled their predecessors in the profession barely two or three decades ago. Leaving aside the many kinds of unethical practices, indulged in by a section of lawyers we find that even some highly successful lawyers seem to live by their own rules of conduct."

Regarding the falling professional standards, this is what the Bench has observed:

> "We express our concern on the falling professional norms among the lawyers with considerable pain because we strongly feel that unless the trend is immediately arrested and reversed, it will have very deleterious consequences for the administration of justice in the country. No judicial system in a democratic society can work satisfactorily unless it is supported by a Bar that enjoys the unqualified trust and confidence of the people, that shares the aspirations, hopes and the ideals of the people and whose members are monetarily accessible affordable to the people."

The image of lawyers would, therefore, depend entirely upon the role which they play in solving the social and other problems facing the country. If the lawyers by showing their professional skills are able to tackle the tasks facing the nation, they would be really playing the role destined for them.

---

1. (2009) 8 SCC 106.

LEGAL PROFESSION—AN INDIAN PERSPECTIVE

"The legal profession is a solemn and serious occupation. It is a noble calling and all those who belong to it are its honourable members. Although the entry to the profession can be had by acquiring merely the qualification of technical competence, the honour as a professional has to be maintained by its members by their exemplary conduct both in and outside the Court. The legal profession is different from other professions in that what the lawyers do, affects not only an individual but the administration of justice, which is the foundation of the civilised society. Both as a leading member of the intelligentsia of the society and as a responsible citizen, the lawyer has to conduct himself as a model for others in his professional, private and public life. The society has a right to expect of him such ideal behaviour".

The legal profession has been aptly summarised by Justice P.B. Sawant in an important judgment of the Supreme Court of India.

Justice V.R. Krishna Iyer in one of the memorable Endowment lectures on "The Constitution, the Court and the Human Rights" says the time has come for, us the legal fraternity, to train our thoughts and change our goals so that lawyers and the legal process may become pivotal to the Constitution.

"All this means that we need a legal profession the Bench and the Bar together committed to the people and the legal system which provides dynamic equality, free legal aid and at least opportunities for securing justice without the hurdles of economic or other disabilities".

Lawyers in India, had played a decisive role not only in the freedom struggle, but in earlier times also in bringing about social awareness among the people. Names of eminent persons come to my mind when I think about the important role which men of law played in modern Indian History. Lawyers have to continue to play a vital role in making India a modern welfare State, say a shining star in the 21st century, among the commity of nations. With the advent of Indian freedom, and enforcement of the Constitution of India, the legal profession has acquired a new mantle. Amongst the four commandments enjoined by the Constitution, the foremost is securing to the citizens justice – social economical and political, and justice and law are synonymous. You cannot think of one without the other. Lawyers' role becomes foremost in fulfilling the Constitutional mandate.

A great lawyer, Johan Davis, way back in 1946 addressed the Association of the Bar of the city of New York with these memorable words:

> "True, we build no bridges. We raise no towers. We construct no pictures.... There is little of all that we do, when the eye of man can see.
>
> But we smooth out difficulties; we relieve stress; we correct mistakes; we take up other men's burdens and by our efforts we make possible the peaceful life of men in a peaceful state".

Very recently the Supreme Court in a case reported as *Satish Kumar* v. *Bar Council of Himachal Pradesh*,[1] states that:

> "the profession of law is called a noble profession. It does not remain noble merely by calling it as such, unless there is a continued corresponding and expected performance of a noble profession. Its nobility has to be preserved, protected and promoted. An institution cannot survive on its name or on its past glory alone. The glory and greatness of an institution depends on its continued and meaningful performance with grace and dignity. The profession of law being noble and an honourable one, it has to continue its meaningful, useful and purposeful performance inspired by and keeping in view the high and rich traditions consistent with its grace, dignity, utility and prestige".

Reference may be made to another case *Rajender V.P. Pai* v. *Alex Fernandes*.[2] The facts of the case were that the appellant, an Advocate on the rolls of Bar Council of Maharashtra and Goa was found guilty of professional misconduct, and his name was directed to be removed from the State Rolls of Advocates. The appeal to the Bar Council of India was also dismissed and the appellant filed an appeal to the Supreme Court under section 38 of the Advocates Act (25/1961). The substance of the allegations found proved was that the appellant solicited professional work from the villagers; that he settled contingent fee depending on the quantum of compensation awarded to the claimant; and that he identified some claimants in opening a bank account wherein the cheque for the awarded amount of compensation was lodged and then the amount withdrawn which identification was later on found to be false.

1. (2001) 2 SCC 365.
2. AIR 2002 SC 1808: (2002) 4 SCC 212.

The Supreme Court did not find any fault or infirmity in the findings recorded about the professional misconduct of the Advocate. However, on the totality of the facts and circumstances of the case, the Supreme Court held that it would meet the ends of justice if the appellant is suspended from the practice for a period of seven years. The Supreme Court, therefore, directed that the license of the Advocate to practice be remained suspended for a period of seven years, instead of the name of the appellant being removed from the rolls of the State Bar Council.

In another case the Bar Council of *Andhra Pradesh* v. *Kurapati Satyanarayana*.[1] The Supreme Court reiterated its view reported in the earlier case of *Harish Chandra Tiwari* v. *Baiju*,[2] and held that "amongst the various types of misconduct envisaged for a legal practitioner the misappropriation of the client's money must be regarded as one of the gravest. It was observed:

> "Among the different types of misconduct envisaged for a legal practitioner misappropriation of the client's money must be regarded as one of the gravest. In his professional capacity the legal practitioner has to collect money from the client towards expenses of the litigation, or withdraw money from the Court payable to the client of take money of the client to be deposited in Court. In all such cases, when the money of the client reaches his hand it is a trust". The Supreme Court affirmed the findings and further held that "having regard to the serious nature of misconduct the punishment of removal of his name from the roll of Bar Council would be the only appropriate punishment and accordingly set aside the other order passed by the Disciplinary Committee of the Bar Council of India and restored that of the Disciplinary Committee of the State Bar Council"

In a very recent case in *Vijay Dhanji Chaudhary* v. *Suhas Jayant Natawadkar*[3], the Hon'ble Supreme Court has taken note of the ongoing rampant unethical practice by some of the Advocates-on- record, duly enrolled under the provisions of the Supreme Court Rules, 1966, as many Special leave Petitions are being filed by them being merely as name-lenders, without having or taking any responsibility for the case.

The aforesaid case is referred in Writ Petition (Civil) 86 of 2010 which was decided on 22-3-2010 titled as *Smt. Poonam* v. *Sumit Tanwar*,[4] in the present case of *inter alia* it was held "the family court, Delhi has passed an order strictly in accordance with law asking the parties to wait for

1. AIR 2003 SC 175: (2003) 1 SCC 102.
2. (2002) 2 SCC 67.
3. (2010) 1 SCC 166.
4. AIR 2010 SC 1384.

statutory period of six months to file the second motion in the case. In such a case fact situation, it is not permissible to suggest that the aforesaid order has violated or infringed any of the fundamental rights or any legal right of the parties. Therefore, we are not able to understand as under what circumstances, the writ is maintainable. The learned counsel appearing for the petitioner is not able to explain under what circumstances, the petition has been filed and as to whether such a petition is maintainable or whether relief of dissolution of marriage could be sought by the parties directly from this court in a case, wherein the marriage had taken place only a year and three months ago".

At para 18 of the judgment the Hon'ble Court referred to the similar issue in *Re*: *Sanjiv Datta*[1], wherein it was observed as under:—

> "Of late, we have been coming across several instances which can only be described as unfortunate both for the legal profession and the administration of justice. It becomes, therefore, our duty to bring it to the notice of the members of the profession that it is in their hands to improve the quality of the service they render both to the litigiant-public and to the courts, and to brighten their image in the society. Some members of the profession have been adopting perceptibly casual approach to the practice of the profession as is evident from their absence when the matters are called out, the filling of incomplete and inaccurate pleadings-many times even illegible and without personal check and verification, the non-payment of court fees and process fees, the failure to remove office objections, the failure to take steps to serve the parties, etc. They do not realize the seriousness of these acts and omissions. They not only amount to the contempt of the court but do positive disservice to the litigants and create embarrassing situation in the court leading to avoidable unpleasantness and delay in the disposal of the matters. This augurs ill for the health of our judicial system...... The legal profession is different from other professions in that what the lawyers do, affects not only an individual but the administration of justice which is the foundation of the civilized society".

The role of a lawyer as approved by the Governing Board of the Union Internationale des Advocates is as under:—

> "Lawyers are by definition part of the legal system in every country. As direct participants in the system of justice, lawyers ensure and maintain the quality of the legal system. Lawyers also play a critical role as counsellor and assistant in accomplishing many commercial and civil transactions. However, clients of lawyers must

1. (1995) 3 SCC 619.

be viewed not only as possible participants in a commercial transaction, but also and more importantly, as citizens who are to be informed, counselled, aided and defended by lawyers who, in so doing, are ensuring the efficient operation of the justice system". [The Indian Advocate Journal of the Bar Association of India, Vol. XXXI (2003)].

The Bar Council, Bar Associations and other organized law groups have to play an important role in fulfilling the aspirations of the people. The bodies must come out with concrete and solid programmes for implementing the constitutional mandates. The programmes must be practical and time bound, and the lawyers should be actively associated with these programmes. The programmes have to be educative and instructive, so that the common people are aware of these, and are in a position to take help.

Another programme of Lawyers' participation is of course the Legal Aid Programmes, which are not being initiated practically in all the States. The Bar Association/Bar Council should also prepare their panel of eminent Advocates, who should be requested to regularly take up these cases on behalf of the Legal Aid Boards which are being set up in States. Where there are no such Legal Aid Boards, the duty falls squarely on the respective Bar Council/Bar Associations to sponsor such Boards, and in their absence to take up this work themselves. With active lawyers' participation only, however, these programmes can get a momentum to achieve the targets set up by the Constitution.

It is the men of character, and integrity among the legal professionals, who can take the lead. Individual lawyers will have to continue to play a pivotal role individually and they cannot escape liability by putting the entire responsibility for the ushering in of a new just order on the State and the respective Bar Councils/Bar Associations.

RULE OF LAW AND ROLE OF LEGAL PROFESSION

On whom does the responsibility to maintain the rule of law lie? Does the judiciary claim to be infallible? On whom does the decision with respect to interpreting and administering the Constitution lie? These are some of the pertinent questions which have been answered by the Supreme Court in a decision cited as *Sanjeev Dutta (in re:)*.[1] Justice P.B. Sawant has analysed the constitutional position regarding the rule of law in the following words:

> "The responsibility to maintain the rule of law lies on all individuals and institutions. Much more, so on the three organs of the State. Our Constitution has separated and demarcated the functions of the Legislature, Executive and Judiciary. Each has to perform functions entrusted to it and respect the functioning of others."

Regarding the infallibility of the judiciary this is what the learned Judge says:

> "None is free from errors, and the judiciary does not claim infallibility. It is truly said that a judge who has not committed a mistake is yet to be born. Our legal system in fact acknowledges the fallibility of the courts and provides for both internal and external checks to correct errors."

The Court referred to the internal checks which are enumerated as the law, the jurisprudence and the precedents, the open public hearing, reasoned judgments, appeals, revisions, references and reviews. The Supreme Court held that among the external checks are objectives, critiques, debates and discussion of judgments outside the courts, and legislative correctives. The Court held that these go a long way to ensure judicial accountability, and the law thus provides procedure to correct judicial errors. The Court held that abuses, attribution of motives, vituperative terrorism and defiance are no methods to correct errors of the Courts. In the discharge of their functions the Courts must be allowed to operate freely and fearlessly but for which impartial adjudication will

1. (1995) 3 SCC 619: JT 1995 (3) SC 538.

be an impossibility. Regarding the authority of the Courts under the Constitution the Supreme Court held as under:—

> "Ours is a Constitutional government based on the rule of law. The Constitution entrusts the task of interpreting and administering the law to the judiciary whose view on the subject is made legally final and binding on all till it is changed by a higher court or by a permissible legislative measure. Those living and functioning under the Constitution have to accept and submit to this obligation of respecting the Constitutional authority of the Courts."

The Court also dealt with the obligations arising out of the practice of the legal profession. The Court held as under:—

> "The legal profession is a solemn and serious occupation. It is a noble calling and all those who belong to it are its honourable members. Although the entry to the profession can be had by acquiring merely the qualification of technical competence, the honour as a professional has to be maintained by its members by their exemplary conduct both in and outside the Court. The legal profession is different from other professions in that what the lawyers do, affect not only an individual but the administration of justice which is the foundation of the civilized society. Both as a leading member of the intelligentsia of the society and as a responsible citizen the lawyer has to conduct himself as a model for others both in his professional and in his private and public life. The society has a right to expect of him such ideal behaviour."

The Court pointed out that the legal profession has always been held in high esteem and its members have played an enviable role in public life. It was further pointed out that the regard for the legal and judicial system in this country is in no small measure due to the tireless role played by the stalwarts in the profession to strengthen them. The Court pointed out the falling standards in the legal profession and said that it is for the members of the profession to introspect and take corrective steps in time. This judgment of the Supreme Court is a landmark judgment as far as the rule of law and role of legal profession is concerned.

Recently the question of lawyers going on strike has been agitating the public mind and the same has been a subject-matter of a number of decisions of the Supreme Court. A Constitution Bench of the Supreme Court has in *Harish Uppal Ex. Capt.* v. *Union of India*,[1] reported, culled out the law in the following terms:—

---

1. (2003) 2 SCC 45.

"Thus the law is already well settled. It is the duty of every Advocate who has accepted a brief to attend trial, even though it may go on day to day for a prolonged period. It is also settled law that a lawyer who has accepted a brief cannot refuse to attend Court because a boycott call is given by the Bar Association. It is settled law that it is unprofessional as well as unbecoming for a lawyer who has accepted a brief to refuse to attend Court even in pursuance of a call for strike or boycott by the Bar Association or the Bar Council. It is settled law that Courts are under an obligation to hear and decide cases brought before it and cannot adjourn matters merely because lawyers are on strike. The law is that it is the duty and obligation of Courts to go on with matters or otherwise it would tantamount to becoming a privy to the strike.........It must also be remembered that an Advocate is an officer of the court and enjoys status in society. Advocates have obligations and duties to ensure smooth functioning of the Court. They owe a duty to their client. Strikes interfere with administration of justice. They cannot thus disrupt court proceedings and put interest of their clients in jeopardy".

This view of the Constitution Bench was reaffirmed by the Hon'ble Supreme Court in a later case *Common Cause A Registered Society* v. *Union of India*.[1]

It was further held as under:—

"That the control of conduct in court can only be within the domain of Courts. Thus article 145 of the Constitution of India gives to the Supreme Court and section 34 of the Advocates Act gives to the High Court power to frame rules including rules regarding condition on which a person (including an Advocate) can practice in the Supreme Court and/or in the High Court and Courts subordinate thereto. Many Courts have framed rules in this behalf".

---

1. AIR 2005 SC 4442.

ROLE OF LAWYERS IN EFFECTING COMPROMISE OF A SUIT*

What is the role of lawyers in effecting compromise in a suit? Is it necessary for a party to sign the agreement of compromise or can a lawyer sign the agreement on behalf of a client? Is there implied authority for a counsel to act on behalf of a client? Is it necessary for a counsel to obtain necessary authority in writing before signing a compromise deed on behalf of his client? These are some of the questions which came up for consideration before the Supreme Court in *Byram Pestonji Gariwala* v. *Union Bank of India.*[1]

The question of law which arose was regarding the construction of Order 23, rule 3, C.P.C. as amended by the Amendment Act of 1976. The Rule with the new proviso added by the Amendment Act reads:

> "Where it is proved to the satisfaction of the Court that a suit has been adjusted wholly or in part by any lawful agreement or compromise, (in writing and signed by the parties) or where the defendant satisfies the plaintiff in respect of the whole or any part of the subject-matter of the suit, the Court shall order such agreement, compromise or satisfaction to be recorded, and shall pass a decree in accordance therewith (so far as it relates to the parties to the suit, whether or not the subject-matter of the agreement, compromise or satisfaction is the same as the subject-matter of the suit):
>
> Provided that where it is alleged by the party and denied by the other that an adjustment or satisfaction had been arrived at, the court shall decide the question; but no adjournment shall be granted for the purpose of deciding the question, unless the court, for reasons to be recorded, thinks fit to grant such adjournment.
>
> *Explanation.*—An agreement or compromise which is void or voidable under the Indian Contract Act, 1872, shall not be deemed to be lawful within the meaning of this rule."

---

* First published in The Indian Advocate; Vol. XXIV, 1992 (January-June), p. 100.

1. JT 1991 (4) SC 15.

The Supreme Court in its latest decision referred to the English Law on this subject and referred to Halsbury's Laws of England, 4th Ed., for the view that the client's consent is not needed for a matter which is within the ordinary authority of a counsel. However, the implied authority of a counsel in England is confined to the matter falling within the subject-matter of the suit. But a compromise is not binding and is liable to be set aside in circumstances which would invalidate any agreement between the parties. The Supreme Court referred to the leading English authorities viz. *Patience Swinfen* v. *Lord Chelmsford*[1]; *Rondel* v. *Worsley*[2] and *Matthews* v. *Munster.*[3]

The Supreme Court in its latest judgment compared the position of counsel in England, Scotland and Ireland with the position of counsel in India in the conduct of cases in Court and referred to the leading cases, *Sheonandan Prasad Singh* v. *V. Hakim Abdul Fateh Mohammad Reza*[4]; *Surendra Nath Mitra* v. *Tarubala Dasi*[5] and Lord Buckmaster in *Hemanta Kumari Debi* v. *Midnapur Zamindari Co.*[6]

The Court reaffirmed the principles laid down in the decision of the Privy Council and other High Courts and in the leading case of *Jamilabai Abdul Kadar* v. *Shankerlal Gulabchand*[7]:

> "Those who know how courts and counsel function will need no education on the jurisprudence of lawyer's position and powers. Of course, we hasten to enter a caveat. It is perfectly open to a party, like any other principal, to mark out in the *vakalatnama* or by particular instructions forbidden areas or expressly withhold the right to act in sensitive matters, the choice being his, as the master. If the lawyer regards these fetters as inconsistent with his position, he may refuse or return the brief. But absent speaking instructions to the contrary, the power to act takes in its wings the right and duty to save a client by settling the suit if and only if he does so *bona fide* in the interests and for the advantage of his client......"

The pronouncement would not have been a landmark judgment but for tracing out the Indian Legal System of judicial administration in its compass. Regarding the Indian legal system the Bench observed as under:

---

1. (1860) 5 H&N 890.
2. (1965) 1 QB 443.
3. (1887) 20 QB 141.
4. AIR 1935 PC 119 (121).
5. AIR 1930 PC 158.
6. AIR 1919 PC 79.
7. (1975) Supp SCR 336 (346).

"The Indian legal system is the product of history. It is rooted in our soil, nurtured and nourished by our culture, languages and traditions; fostered and sharpened by our genius and quest for social justice, reinforced by history and heritage; it is not a mere copy of the English common law; though inspired and strengthened, guided and enriched by concepts and precepts of justice, equity and good conscience which are indeed the hall-mark of the common law".

In the words of M.C. Setalvad, J. "The massive structure of Indian Law and jurisprudence resembles the height, the symmetry and the grandeur of the common and statute law of England...".

Regarding judicial administration and the amendment in Order 23 rule 3, C.P.C. the Court observed:

"In our own system of judicial administration if strains have developed and cracks have appeared by the stresses and pressures of the time; if aberrations have become too obvious to be ignored or too deep-rooted to be corrected by an internal mechanism; if the traditional role of the legal profession requires urgent legislative scrutiny with a view to remedying the defects and strengthening and safeguarding the system; it is a matter exclusively for Parliament to consider; but the amendment in question is not addressed to that purpose."

The Court accordingly held that the words 'in writing and signed by the parties' inserted by C.P.C. (Amendment Act) of 1976 must necessarily mean "any appearance, application or act in or to any court, required or authorized by law to be made or done by a party in such court, may, except where otherwise expressly provided by any law for the time being in force, be made or done by the party in person, *or by his recognized agent, or by a pleader,* appearing, applying or acting as the case may be, on his behalf."

Accordingly, the Supreme Court held that the decree passed by the High Court on 18 June, 1984 in terms of the compromise was a valid decree and it constituted *res judicata*. The court relied on the ratio of the decisions referred to in *Shankar Sitaram Sontakke* v. *Bal Krishna Sitaram Sontakke*[1]; *Sailendra Narayan Bhanja Deo* v. *State of Orissa*[2] and *Mohanlal Goenka* v. *Benoy Krishna Mukherjee*.[3]

The court, however, sounded a note of caution, which would be useful for lawyers to heed:

1. AIR 1954 SC 352.
2. AIR 1956 SC 346.
3. AIR 1953 SC 65.

"We may, however, hasten to add that it will be prudent for counsel not to act on implied authority except when warranted by the exigency of circumstances demanding immediate adjustment of suit by agreement or compromise and the signature of the party cannot be obtained without undue delay. In these days of easier and quicker communication, such contingency may seldom arise. A wise and careful counsel will no doubt arm himself in advance with the necessary authority expressed in writing to meet all such contingencies in order that neither his authority nor integrity is ever doubted. This essential precaution will safeguard the personal reputation of counsel as well as uphold the prestige and dignity of the legal profession".

The court further held as under:—

"To insist upon the party himself personally signing the agreement or compromise would often cause undue delay, loss and inconvenience, especially in the case of non-resident persons. It has always been universally understood that a party can always act by him duly authorized representative. If a power of attorney holder can enter into an agreement or compromise on behalf of his principal, so can counsel, possessed of the requisite authorization by vakalatnama, act on behalf of his client. Not to recognize such capacity is not only to cause much inconvenience and loss to the parties personally, but also to delay the progress of proceedings in Court:".

The Supreme Court had occasion to consider the matter in the latest ruling reported as *Jineshwardas* v. *Jagrani*.[1] The above referred principles of law were reiterated in the said judgment in the following manner:—

"We are in respectful agreement with the above statement of law. Consequently it is not permissible for the appellant, to contend to the contrary".

On the facts of the case the Supreme Court further held as under:—

"That apart we are also of the view that a judgment or decree passed as result of consensus arrived at before Court, cannot always be said to be one passed on compromise or settlement and adjustment. It may, at times, be also a judgment on admission, as in this case".

This case has been referred to in a later decision of the Supreme Court reported as *Pushpa Devi Bhagat* v. *Rajinder Singh*.[2] It was *inter-alia* held that

1. AIR 2003 SC 4596.
2. AIR 2006 SC 2628.

to "to insist upon the party himself personally signing the agreement or compromise would often cause undue delay, loss and inconvenience, especially in the case of non-resident persons. It has always been universally understood that a party can always act by his duly authorised representative. If a power-of-attorney holder can enter into an agreement or compromise on behalf of his principal, so can counsel, possessed of the requisite authorisation by vakalatnama, act on behalf of his client... If the legislature had intended to make such a fundamental change, even at the risk of delay, inconvenience and needless expenditure, it would have expressly so stated."

PART II

LAW AND JUDICIARY

LAW AND JUDICIARY

JUDICIAL ACTIVISM

The phenomenon of Judicial Activism has assumed great significance during recent times. The latest judgments of the Supreme Court have drawn the attention of the entire nation to the role of judicial activism undertaken by the Supreme Court of the country. The landmark judgment of the Supreme Court, upholding the expulsion of 12 MPs, delivered on Wednesday the 10th January, 2007, although, endorsing the Parliament's decision to expel 12 MPs stung by the cash for query and the Members of Parliament LAND scams, but asserts for itself the role to play the final arbiter by sitting in judgment on the legality of the decision taken by the legislature. The judgment of the 5 Judges Bench was not an unanimous one with Mr. Justice R.V. Raveendran dissenting.

The majority 357-page judgment on the petition of expelled MPs challenging Parliament's power to expel its members has two parts. The first one validates the decision of Parliament to terminate the membership of those who were caught on camera accepting money for putting questions. The Court was unambiguous that article 105(3) confers on Parliament the right to punish, including expulsion of an errant member.

There is, however, the other part of the verdict which is fraught with long-term repercussions for the judiciary-legislature inter-play, which may not be liked by the Parliamentarians. In an emphatic statement of the judiciary's claim to be the final arbiter, the Court said that it had the constitutional competence to examine the legality of the decisions taken by the Parliament if they smacked of *mala fide* or infringement of fundamental rights.

The judgment subjects Parliamentary action to judicial review and holds that the Supreme Court is the final arbiter for testing the legality of any action and judicial scrutiny is permissible of tainted or illegal Parliamentary proceedings. The judgment will classify itself to be called a landmark judgment. The two Constitutional Experts *viz.* former Attorney General, Soli, J. Sorabjee and Senior Advocate Fali Nariman have saluted the verdict bestowing the Parliament with power to expel MPs, saying that it was a "statesman-like decision". Both the

Constitutional Experts agreed with the Court's decision that judiciary is the ultimate authority to test the legality of the manner in which such power was exercised.

The second landmark judgment is wherein the Supreme Court held that the laws in the Ninth Schedule are open to judicial scrutiny. The Supreme Court on 11th of January, 2007 held that the laws put in the Ninth Schedule after April, 1973 cannot escape judicial scrutiny if they appeared to breach citizens' fundamental rights or undermine the basic structure of the Constitution.

The unanimous verdict by the nine-Judge Constitution Bench led by Chief Justice Y.K. Sabharwal, like the earlier one by the Apex Court in the MPs' expulsion case, asserted the Court's role as the final arbiter at the expense of the notions of Parliamentary supremacy, expanding the frontiers of judicial review.

The effects of this judgment is going to be far reaching as many crucial laws, including the law enacted by the Tamil Nadu to extend reservation well beyond the Supreme Court mandate of 50% ceiling, would now be open to challenge in the courts, on the ground of being contrary to the basic structure as well as violating the fundamental rights. In a nutshell a nine-Judge Bench of the Supreme Court headed by Chief Justice Y.K. Sabharwal said that right to equality (Articles 14, 15 and 16), right to freedom of speech and expression (Articles 19) and right to life (Article 21) with all their extended interpretations form the core of the Constitution, which could by no means be violated by Parliament's amending power.

The above noted judgments have highlighted the important role played by the Supreme Court during the recent times.

Before we take note of these pronouncements, it would be necessary to mention that the Indian judiciary with the Supreme Court at the apex has been playing the role of an activist judiciary for the past many decades. The phenomenon is referred to as Judicial Activism. The Supreme Court has been delivering landmark judgments in respect of article 21 of the Constitution of India. The landmark judgments were all examples of Judicial Activism and may be summaried as below:—

(1) The right to go abroad. *Satwant Singh Sawhney* v. *D. Ramarathanam APO, New Delhi;*[1]

(2) The right to privacy. *Govind* v. *State of Madhya Pradesh*[2]. In this case reliance was placed on the American decision in *Griswold* v. *Connecticut;*[3]

1. AIR 1967 SC 1836.
2. 1975 Cr LJ 1111: AIR 1975 SC 1378.
3. (1965) 381 US 479.

(3) The right against solitary confinement. *Sunil Batra* v. *Delhi Administration;*[1]

(4) The right against the fetters. *Charles Shobraj* v. *Supdt. Central Jail;*[2]

(5) The right to legal aid. *M.H. Hoskot* v. *State of Maharashtra;*[3]

(6) The right to speedy trial. *Hussainara Khatoon* v. *Home Secretary, State of Bihar;*[4]

(7) The right against handcuffing. *Prem Shankar Shukla* v. *Delhi Administration;*[5]

(8) The right against delayed execution. *T.V. Vatheeswaran* v. *State of Tamil Nadu;*[6]

(9) The right against custodial violence. *Sheela Barse* v. *State of Maharashtra*[7]

(10) The right against public hanging. *A.G. of India* v. *Lachma Devi;*[9]

(11) Doctor's assistance. *Parmanand Katara* v. *Union of India;*[9]

(12) Shelter. *Shantistar Builders* v. *N.K. Totame;*[10]

(13) The right of arrestee. *D.K. Basu* v. *State of West Bengal;*[11]

(14) The right of the female employees not to be sexually harassed at the place of work. *Vishakha* v. *State of Rajasthan;*[12] and

(15) *Apparel Export Promotion Council* v. *A.K. Chopra.*[13]

The further intervention of the Supreme Court had been in the matter awarding compensation in the cases where the persons had been detained illegally and where there was violation of fundamental rights. In the leading case of *Rudul Sah* v. *State of Bihar,*[14] the Court granted compensation and rehabilitation for victims deprived of their fundamental rights. There have been numerous other cases of award of

1. AIR 1978 SC 1675: (1978) Cr LJ 1741.
2. AIR 1978 SC 1514: (1978) Cr LJ 1534.
3. AIR 1978 SC 1548: (1978) Cr LJ 1678.
4. AIR 1979 SC 1360: (1979) Cr LJ 1036.
5. AIR 1980 SC 1535: (1980) Cr LJ 930: (1980) 3 SCC 526.
6. AIR 1983 SC 361 (2): (1983) Cr LJ 481.
7. AIR 1983 SC 378: (1983) Cr LJ 642.
8. AIR 1986 SC 467: (1986) Cr LJ 364.
9. AIR 1989 SC 2039: (1990) Cr LJ 671.
10. AIR 1990 SC 630.
11. (1997) 1 SCC 416.
12. (1997) 6 SCC 241.
13. JT 1999 (1) SC 61.
14. AIR 1983 SC 1086: (1983) 3 SCR 508.

compensation and giving other remedial relief in cases of breach of fundamental rights in appropriate cases. Reference may be made to *M.C. Mehta* v. *Union of India*[1]; *Nilabati Behera* v. *State of Orissa*[2]; etc. These judgments point out the fact that judicial activism is not a recent phenomenon and the courts have been exercising their powers in a manner that may be called an exercise in judicial activism. Traces of judicial activism can be found even in earlier judgments.

There have recently been some outbursts against the role of judiciary in interfering with the matters that pertain to the Executive and the Legislature. Soli Sorabjee rightly pointed out that "Indignant critics forget that it is the executive's failure to perform its duty and the notorious tardiness of the Legislature that impels judicial activism and provides it motivation and legitimacy. When gross violations of human rights are brought to its notice, the judiciary cannot procrastinate. It must respond."

The former Hon'ble Chief Justice of India, A.M. Ahmedi is also reported to have said in his Zakir Hussain Memorial Lecture that the phenomenon of judicial activism in its aggressive role will have to be a temporary one. Former Hon'ble Chief Justice of India, Adarsh Sein Anand has stoutly defended judicial activism saying that the expanded role of judiciary has received acceptability not only by the people but by other wings of the State as well.

Speaking at the SAARC Law Conference at Colombo, he said that the criticism notwithstanding, our experience is that the activist role of judiciary, used with proper self-restraint, is desirable for the general good of the people, for whom the courts of law ultimately exist. There is, therefore, no need to treat this exercise as an attempt by the judiciary to either clutch at the jurisdiction or to usurp the function of any other organ of the State. He, however, has given a word of caution in his inaugural address for the Millennium Law Lecture Series at Kochi, Kerala on October 21, 1999.

Judicial activism, however, is not an unguided missile. It has to be controlled and properly channelised. Courts have to function within established parameters and constitutional bounds. Decision should have a jurisprudential base with clearly discernible principles. Limits of jurisdiction cannot be pushed back so as to make them irrelevant. Courts have to be careful to see that they do not overstep their limits because to them is assigned the sacred duty of guarding the Constitution. People of this country have reposed faith and trust in the courts and, therefore, the

1. AIR 1997 SC 1986.
2. AIR 1993 SC 1960.

judges have to act as their trustees. Betrayal of that trust would lead to judicial despotism, which posterity would not forgive.

Regarding the scope of Judicial Activism in matters relating to prescribing the period of limitation, the Constitution Bench of Supreme Court in a case *Ramachandra Rao* v. *State of Karnataka*[1], has held as under:—

> "Prescribing periods of limitation at the end of which the trial court would be obliged to terminate the proceedings and necessarily acquit or discharge the accused, and further, making such directions applicable to all the cases in the present and for the future amounts to legislation, which, cannot be done by judicial directives and within the arena of the judicial law-making power available to constitutional courts, howsoever liberally articles 21, 32, 141 and 142 of the Constitution may be interpreted.
>
> The primary function of the judiciary is to interpret the law. It may lay down principles, guidelines and exhibit creativity in the field left open and unoccupied by legislation. Courts can declare the law, they can interpret the law, they can remove obvious lacunae and fill the gaps but they cannot entrench upon in the field of legislation properly meant for the Legislature".

The matters relating to right of Educational Institutions to establish and run their institutions came up for hearing before the constitutional Bench of Supreme Court in a case *P.A. Inamdar* v. *State of Maharashtra*[2] has held as under:—

> "It is for the Central Government, or for the State Governments, in the absence of a Central legislation, to come out with a detailed well thought out legislation on the subject. Such legislation is long awaited. The States must act towards this direction. The judicial wing of the State is called upon the act when the other two wings, the Legislature and the Executive, do not act. The earlier the Union of India and the State Governments act, the better it would be".

The scope of judicial activism pertaining to public employment came up for hearing before the Supreme Court in a case *Indian Drugs & Pharmaceuticals Ltd.* v. *Workmen*[3] has held as under:—

> "Orders for creation of posts, appointment on these posts, regularization, fixing pay scales, continuation in service, promotions, etc., are all Executive or Legislative functions, and it is highly

1. AIR 2002 SC 1856.
2. AIR 2005 SC 3226.
3. (2007) 1 SCC 408.

> improper for judges to step into this sphere, except in a rare and exceptional case. The courts must exercise judicial restraint in this connection, and not encroach into the Executive or Legislative domain. The tendency in some courts/tribunals to Legislate or perform Executive functions cannot be appreciated. Judicial activism in some extreme and exceptional situations can be justified, but resorting to it readily and frequently, as has latterly been happening, is not only unconstitutional, it is also fraught with grave peril for the judiciary."

Creation and abolition of posts and regularization are purely Executive functions. Hence, the court cannot create a post where none exists. Also the Supreme Court cannot issue directions to absorb the respondents or continue them in service, or pay them salaries of regular employees, as these are purely Executive functions. The Supreme Court cannot arrogate to itself the powers of the Executive or Legislature. There is broad separation of powers under the Constitution, and the judiciary, too, must know its limits".

Examples of Judicial activism are mostly manifest in "what is known as Public Interest Litigation" initiated by individuals and or groups seeking courts intervention.

In a recent case the complete parameters to entertain PIL have been laid down by the Hon'ble Mr. Justice Dalveer Bhandari, and Hon'ble Dr. M.K. Sharma, J. of Supreme Court on January 18, 2010, titled as *State of Uttaranchal* v. *Balwant Singh Chaufal*.[1] The earlier judgments of the Supreme Court have been analyzed. Ultimately, the Supreme Court has held as under:—

> "181. We have carefully considered the facts of the present case. We have also examined the law declared by this Court and other courts in a number of judgments. In order to preserve the purity and sanctity of the PIL, it has become imperative to issue the following directions:—
>
> (1) The courts must encourage genuine and *bona fide* PIL and effectively discourage and curb the PIL filed for extraneous considerations.
>
> (2) Instead of every individual Judge devising his own procedure for dealing with the public interest litigation, it would be appropriate for each High Court to properly formulate rules for encouraging the genuine PIL and discouraging the PIL filed with oblique motives. Consequently, we request that the High

1. (2010) 3 SCC 402.

Courts who have not yet framed the rules, should frame the rules within three months. The Registrar General of each High Court is directed to ensure that a copy of the rules prepared by the High Court is sent to the Secretary General of this Court immediately thereafter.

(3) The courts should *prima facie* verify the credentials of the petitioner before entertaining a PIL...

(4) The Courts should be *prima facie* satisfied regarding the correctness of the contents of the petition before entertaining a PIL.

(5) The courts should be fully satisfied that substantial public interest is involved before entertaining the petition.

(6) The Courts should ensure that the petition which involves larger public interest, gravity and urgency must be given priority over other petitions.

(7) The Courts before entertaining the PIL should ensure that the PIL is aimed at redressal of genuine public harm or public inquiry. The court should also ensure that there is no personal gain, private motive or oblique motive behind filing the public interest litigation.

(8) The Courts should also ensure that the petitions filed by busybodies for extraneous and ulterior motives must be discouraged by imposing exemplary costs or by adopting similar novel methods to curb frivolous petitions and the petitions filed for extraneous considerations.

182. Copies of this judgment be sent to the Registrar General of all the High Courts within one week."

It appears that at least for some more time the country is going to face judicial activism of the courts, which, as earlier pointed out, has been necessitated on account of failure of the Executive and the Legislature and till such time the Executive and the Legislatures come up to the high standard that is required and expected of them, judicial activism will continue to play an important role in the affairs of the nation.

JUDICIAL ACCOUNTABILITY/NORMS FOR CONDUCT OF JUDGES

Some of the recent events in this country have raised the question of accountability of Judges and matters relating to appointments, transfers, impeachment and taking other steps for controlling the alleged misconduct of the Judges. I may make reference to the misconduct of the Gujarat High Court Judges, which led to transfer of the two Judges of the Gujarat High Court.

The then Chief Justice Y.K. Sabharwal on the eve of his retirement also said that he had been deeply hurt by the media reports on the fist blows given by a Gujarat High Court Judge to his colleague. The Chief Justice of India, Y.K. Sabharwal also hinted that the Apex Court collegium is contemplating suitable action, as the incident sullied the image of the judiciary. This was followed by the news of transfer of the two Judges to other High Court *viz.* the transfers of Mr. Justice B.J. Shethna to Sikkim High Court and of Mr. Justice P.B Majumdar to Rajasthan High Court.

The second news item concerning the judiciary is the news of Mr. Justice Bhalla's elevation as Chief Justice of Kerala High Court. In another news item of the Times of India edition of February 11, 2007 under the heading "Govt.-Kalam ties fraying at edges – Bhalla's Elevation Row is the Third such instance of clash between the two – Trouble at the Top" has reported as under:

> "The President's decision to signal his unhappiness over Justice Bhalla's elevation, apparently in the light of controversy surrounding acquisition of a Noida plot by his wife, is the third instance of Kalam taking a less than sanguine view of government decisions in the last year-and-a-half". Another news item appeared in the newspaper of the same date under the heading "Bhardwaj downplays row over judges elevation and quoted the statement of the Hon'ble Law Minister, who termed it as a part of consultation process without reading more into it.

Another important news was about the report of the Administrative Reforms Commission, headed by Mr. Veerappa Moily, who has made adverse comments about the recently introduced Judges (Inquiry) Bill, 2006 introduced by the Law Minister in the last session of Parliament, which leaves it entirely to the Judges to deal with the complaints of judicial misconduct. The Administrative Reforms Commission has suggested that the composition of the National Judicial Council needs to be broad based and its powers enhanced so that it could exercise the foresight of the judiciary. The Commission has relied on the composition existing in the US and the UK and suggested that the members of the Council should be "in line with universally accepted principles, and be headed by the Vice-President and consist of the Prime Minister, Speaker, Chief Justice of India, Law Minister and leaders of the Opposition in the two Houses. The Commission has also suggested that the members of the Council should be empowered not only to impose minor measures but also recommend removal in serious cases of judicial misconduct.

The Times of India in its Editorial of 14th February, 2007 has welcomed Moily Panel's proposal in the following words:—

> "The proposal to set up a National Judicial Council (NJC), which will decide on the appointment and removal of Judges, is an improvement on the Judges (Inquiry) Bill drafted by the Union Law Ministry. The Law Ministry Bill has called for an NJC constituted exclusively of members of the judiciary. The Moily Commission wants the council to be more broad based. It seeks to include the members of the legislature and the executive besides Judges in the council. The suggestion is welcomed. The Commission for judicial appointments in the UK is constituted of eminent professionals who have never been lawyers or held any judicial office. A more representative NJC would only reinforce the impartial character of the judiciary. The suggestion need not be read as a vote against the current practice of sitting Judges selecting their peers".

These recent developments, have again focussed the attention on the questions relating to the accountability of the judiciary.

Let us examine now the existing provisions regarding the conduct of the Judges under the Constitution.

Reference may be made to articles 121, 124 and 217 of the Constitution of India.

Article 121 specifically provides that "no discussion shall take place in Parliament with respect to the conduct of any Judge of the Supreme Court or of a High Court in the discharge of his duties expect upon a motion for presenting an address to the President praying for the removal of the Judge".

Article 124(4) dealing with removal of a Supreme Court Judge provides that "a Judge of the Supreme Court shall not be removed from his office except by an order of the President passed after an address by each House of Parliament supported by a majority of the total membership of that House and by a majority of not less than two-thirds of the members of the House present and voting has been presented to the President in the same session for such removal on the ground of proved misbehaviour or incapacity".

Article 127 (b) provides that a High Court Judge be removed from his office by the President in the same manner as provided under article 124(4) for removal of a Supreme Court Judge.

Recent events have shown that the existing provisions in the Constitution are totally inadequate to deal with the cases of delinquent Judges.

The Law Commission of India, in their one hundred and twenty-first Report also, emphasized the need for a change in the system, and the Constitution (Amendment) Bill, 1996, provided for the creation of a National Judicial Commission, but the Bill did not see the light of the day. However, it is noteworthy to study some of the salient provisions in the recently introduced Bill No. 97 of 2006, called the Judges (Inquiry) Bill, 2006.

The Statement of Objects and Reasons states that "a suitable legislative framework is the need of the hour for empowering a judicial forum to deal with complaints against Judges of the Supreme Court and High Courts. On the basis of the recommendations made in the 195th Report of the Law Commission of India on the Judges (Inquiry) Bill, 2005, the Bill, namely the Judges (Inquiry) Bill, 2006 has been prepared". It further provides that "the Bill, namely, the Judges (Inquiry) Bill, 2006 is based on the premise that judicial independence is one of the basic fundamentals of the Constitution. Judicial independence and judicial accountability are inseparable. Thus, there is an urgent need of a legislation for establishing a National Judicial Council to look into the allegations of misbehaviour or incapacity of a Judge of the Supreme Court or of a High Court, as the case may be, and to regulate the procedure for such investigation, inquiry and proof in a complaint procedure in addition to the earlier "reference procedure" as contained in the Judges (Inquiry) Act, 1968."

Section 2(f) defines incapacity as under:—

> "Incapacity" means physical or mental incapacity which is or is likely to be of a permanent character".

Section 2(i) defines misbehavour as under:—

> "Misbehaviour" means wilful or persistent conduct which brings dishonour or disrepute to the judiciary; or wilful or persistent failure to perform the duties of a Judge; or wilful abuse of judicial office, corruption, lack of integrity, or committing an offence involving moral turpitude; and includes violation of Code of Conduct".

Section 3 provides for establishment of a National Judicial Commission which shall consist of the following:—

(a) The Chief Justice of India - Chairman

(b) Two senior-most Judges of the Supreme Court, to be nominated by the Chief Justice of India - Members

(c) Two Chief Justices of the High Courts, to be nominated by the Chief Justice of India - Members

Section 5(1) provides that "it shall be the duty of the National Judicial Council to investigate and inquire into any matter involving, or arising from, or connected with, any allegation of misbehaviour or incapacity against a Judge of the Supreme Court or a Judge of a High Court, as the case may be."

Section 7 provides for the appointment of staff of the Council.

Section 9 provides for the verification and preliminary investigation of complaints by the Council.

Section 10 provides for the procedure in respect of inquiries and provides as under:—

> "If after the verification and preliminary investigation under section 9 in respect of a complaint, the Council proposes to conduct an inquiry, it shall frame definite charges against the Judge on the basis of which the inquiry is proposed to be held.
>
> Charges framed under sub-section (1) together with the statement of grounds on which each such charge is based shall be communicated to the Judge and he shall be given a reasonable opportunity of presenting a written statement of defence within such time as may be specified by the Council".

Section 13 provides for the procedure of Enquiry in case of Physical or mental incapacity of a Judge.

Section 14 provides that inquiry is to be conducted *in camera* by the Chairman and the members of the Council sitting jointly.

Section 20(1)(a) provides that if the Council is satisfied that "no charges have been proved, it shall dismiss the complaint and no further action shall be taken against the Judge and the Judge and the complainant shall be informed accordingly".

Section 20(1)(b) provides that if all or any of the charges in regard to misbehaviour or incapacity have been proved and the Council is of the opinion that the charges proved do not warrant removal of the Judge, it may impose all or any of the following minor measures, namely:—

(i) Issuing advisories;

(ii) Issuing warnings;

(iii) Withdrawing of Judicial work for a limited time including cases already assigned;

(iv) Request that the Judge may voluntarily retire;

(v) Censure or admonition, public or private.

Section 27 provides for a complete confidentiality in complaint procedure.

Section 29 provides for the stoppage of assigning judicial work during the pendency of the preliminary investigation or inquiry or address by the House to the President.

Section 30 provides for appeal to the Supreme Court by the aggrieved Judge.

Section 36 provides for the Code of Conduct of Judges as under:—

"(1) The Council shall, in the interests of administration of justice, issue from time to time, a Code of Conduct containing guidelines for the conduct and behaviour of Judges.

(2) Till the Code of Conduct referred to in sub-section (1) is issued, "The Restatement of Values of Judicial Life adopted by the Chief Justices' Conference of India, 1999", shall be the Code of Conduct for the purposes of this Act.

(3) The Code of Conduct issued under sub-section (1) may, *inter alia,* provide that every Judge at the time of appointment as a Judge of the Supreme Court or of the High Court and thereafter shall annually give intimation of his assets and liabilities to the Chief Justice of India or the Chief Justice of the High Court, as the case may be.

(4) The Code of Conduct shall be published in the Official Gazette and the Council shall in the like manner amend the said Code from time to time".

I propose to deal with some of the important aspects of the Judges (Inquiry) Bill, 2006. The first and foremost question is about the composition of the members of the Judicial Council. Under the present

Bill, only the members of the judiciary (CJI, two Senior Judges of the Supreme Court and two Judges of the High Court), are members of the Council. Should it be as broad based as suggested by the Report of the Administrative Reforms Commission, headed by Veerappa Moily, as earlier referred to *viz.* headed by the Vice-President and consisting of the Prime Minister, Speaker, Chief Justice of India, Law Minister, and Leader of the Opposition in the two Houses? The same in my opinion would be too broad based, and may lead to political interference and may hamper the independence of the judiciary.

In my opinion, it would be advisable to have at least one member from the members of the Bar *viz.* an outstanding Senior Advocate commanding universal respect for learning and integrity, apart from the one's suggested in the Bill. The Bar is also an important part of the judicial administration and the association of an eminent member of the Bar would go a long way in making the Council sufficiently broad based.

The second important aspect is the one related to complaint procedure. The 1st proviso to clause 8, which restricts the scope of the enquiry to only acts and/or conduct constituting misbehaviour, which have taken place subsequent to the commencement of the Act, in my opinion, should be removed. The other proviso, providing for limiting the enquiry to a period of 2 years, prior to the filing of the complaint, may, however, be retained. The limitation of 2 or 3 years appears to be reasonable and sound.

The third important aspect is the one relating to disposal of complaint and the follow up action provided under section 20 of the Bill. The minor penalties or minor measures recommended in respect of the charges proved, also require to be re-examined. The measure of issuing advisories under clause 29(b)(i) requires clarification as to the nature and scope of advisories. Will the same be public or private? Similarly, in case of issuing warnings, under clause (b)(ii), will the same be public or private?

The fourth important aspect is section 36, providing for code of conduct for Judges, which shall contain guidelines for the conduct and behaviour of the Judges. For the interim period, till the code of conduct is issued, section 36(2) provides that the Restatement of values of judicial life, adopted by the Chief Justices' Conference of India, 1999, shall be the code of conduct. However, the same are neither readily available, nor are they known to the public. These are not even known to the majority of the members of the Bar. It would, therefore, be advisable to have the same incorporated in the Bill.

In my opinion, the provisions of section 23, imposing disqualifications of the removed Judge, confidentiality in complaint procedure (section 27) and provision relating to the stoppage of judicial work in certain cases, are welcome steps in the new Bill.

On the whole, I am in respectful agreement with the views of eminent Senior Advocates, Fali Nariman and Dr. Abhishek Singhvi regarding the utility of the Bill. The proposed Bill is, generally speaking, a desirable step in the right direction for sustaining and enhancing respect for the judiciary.

CRITERIA FOR SELECTION AND TRANSPARENCY IN APPOINTMENT OF JUDGES*

The independence of judiciary, which is one of the basic pillars of democracy, is closely linked with the issue of the appointment of Judges. The Supreme Court of India has time and again emphasised this aspect in its various judgments in the following words:

> "Needless to say that the independence, efficiency and integrity of the judiciary can only be maintained by selecting the best persons in accordance with the procedure provided under the Constitution. The objectives enshrined in the Constitution cannot be achieved unless the functionaries accountable for making appointments act with meticulous care and utmost responsibility."

Regarding the judicial process, and role of Judges, it is said:

> "The nature of the judicial process is such that under coercive winds the flame of justice flickers, faints and fades, the true Judge is one who should be beyond purchase by threat or temptation popularity or prospects. To float with the tide is easy, to counter the counterfeit current is uneasy and yet Judge must be ready for it."

The reference at this stage may be made to the provision of the Constitution of India. Article 50 of the Constitution provides for separation of Judiciary from Executive. Article 50 is quoted below:

> "The State shall take steps to separate the Judiciary from the Executive in the public services of the State."

Chapter IV of Part V of the Indian Constitution provides for the Union Judiciary. Article 124 provides for establishment and Constitution of the Supreme Court, article 126 provides for the appointment of Acting Chief Justices, article 127 provides for the appointment of *ad hoc* Judges and article 129 provides "that the Supreme Court shall be a Court of record and shall have all the powers of such a Court including the power to punish for contempt of itself."

---

* A paper presented in seminar on *appointment of Judges* organised by The Bar Association of India, 17-18 September, 1999, p. 114.

The conditions of eligibility of Supreme Court Judge is provided in article 124(3) as under:

> "A person shall not be qualified for appointment as a Judge of the Supreme Court unless he is a citizen of India, and
>
> (a) has been for at least five years a Judge of a High Court or of two or more such Courts in succession; or
>
> (b) has been for at least ten years an advocate of a High Court or of two or more such Courts in succession; or
>
> (c) is, in the opinion of the President, a distinguished jurist."

Similarly, Chapter V of Part IV of the Constitution of India provides for the High Courts in the States. Article 215 provides that "every High Court shall be a court of record and shall have all the powers of such a Court including the power to punish for contempt of itself."

The appointment and condition of the office of a Judge of a High Court is provided under article 217. The conditions of the eligibility are as follows:

> "A person shall not be qualified for appointment as a Judge of a High Court unless he is a citizen of India, and
>
> (a) has for at least ten years held a judicial office in the territory of India; or
>
> (b) has for at least ten years been an advocate of a High Court or of two or more such Courts in succession."

It is apparent that the minimum qualification for the appointment of Judge leaves wide choice and a suitable mechanism has to be evolved for the appointment of a person of merits as a Judge of the Supreme Court and/or High Courts. Similarly, even for the appointment of Judges for subordinate judiciary, who also play an important role in administration of justice the choice is very wide and it is essential that the selection process should be such that the men of merits and integrity alone are appointed as Judges.

The aspect of appointment of Judges will be incomplete without a reference to the judgment of the Supreme Court in *S.P. Gupta* v. *Union of India*[1], a case decided by seven Judges of the Supreme Court. Mr. Justice Bhagwati in his judgment referred to the quotation of Mr. Justice Krishna Iyer in the following words:

> "Appointment of Judges is a serious process where judicial expertise, legal learning, life's experience and high integrity are components, but above all are two indispensables—social

1. AIR 1982 SC 149.

philosophy in active Unison with the socialistic Articles of the Constitution, and the second but equally important, built-in resistance to pushes and pressures by class interests, private prejudices, Government threats and blandishments, party loyalties and contrary economic and political ideologies projecting into pronouncements."

It is useful to point out to the role assigned to the Judges by Justice Bhagwati in the following words:

> "What is necessary is to have Judges who are prepared to fashion new tools, forge new methods, innovate new strategies and evolve a new jurisprudence, who are judicial statesmen with a social vision and a creative faculty and who have, above all, a deep sense of commitment to the Constitution with an activist approach and obligation for accountability not to any party in power nor to the opposition nor to the classes which are vociferous but to the half hungry millions of Indians who are continually denied their basic human rights. We need Judges who are alive to the socio-economic realities of Indian life who are anxious to wipe every tear from every eye, who have faith in the constitutional values and who are ready to use law as an instrument for achieving the constitutional objectives."

In the above referred judgment, reference has also been made to the practices existing in other countries with respect to appointment of Judges. In England Judges are appointed by the Executive. Nevertheless, the judiciary is substantially insulated by virtue of rules of strict law, constitutional conventions political practice and professional tradition from political influence (Halsbury's Laws of England, 4th Edn., Vol. 1, para 5).

In Australia the Justices of the High Court and of the other courts created by the Parliament are appointed by the Governor-General in Council [*See* section 72(1) of the Commonwealth of Australia Constitution Act, 1900]. The appointment of federal Judges is a Cabinet matter which is formally ratified by the Executive Council. It is stated that the practice is that the Attorney-General would recommend to Cabinet persons for appointment though it is the Cabinet which will make the final decision.

In Japan the Emperor appoints the Chief Justice of the Supreme Court as designated by the Cabinet and Judges other than the Chief Justice are appointed by the Cabinet.

The *S.P. Gupta* case had come up for reconsideration in *Supreme Court Advocates on Record Association* v. *Union of India*[1], wherein the earlier

1. AIR 1994 SC 268.

judgment was overruled and it was held that the opinion of the Chief Justice of India (CJI) has primacy in the matter of appointment of the Judges of High Courts and the Supreme Court. The method of appointment of Judges prevailing in the various other countries was also discussed in this judgment (*i.e.*, of American system, Australian system, Canadian system and the New Zealand system).

The summary of the conclusions is given at page 442 of the judgment and briefly given as under:

(a) The process of appointment of Judges to the Supreme Court and the High Courts is an integrated 'participatory consultative process' for selecting the best and most suitable person's available for appointment and all the constitutional functionaries must perform this duty collectively with a view primarily to reach an agreed decision, subserving the constitutional purpose, so that the occasion of primacy does not arise;

(b) No appointment of any Judge to the Supreme Court or any High Court can be made, unless it is in conformity with the opinion of the Chief Justice of India; and

(c) Only limited judicial review on the grounds specified earlier is available in matters of appointments and transfers.

Ultimately a reference was also made to the Supreme Court by the President of India on 23-7-1998. The reference came up for hearing before a Constitution Bench of 9 Judges of the Hon'ble Supreme Court, and the Supreme Court answered the reference by reiterating the earlier decisions and clarifying the process for appointment of judges. The case is reported as AIR 1999 SC 1 in Special Reference No. 1 of 1998, dated 28-10-1998. The Hon'ble Supreme Court *inter alia* held as under:—

(1) The expression "consultation with the Chief Justice of India" in articles 217(1) and 222(1) of the Constitution of India requires consultation with a plurality of Judges in the formation of the opinion of the Chief Justice of India. The sole, individual opinion of the Chief Justice of India does not constitute "consultation" within the meaning of the said article.

(2) The Chief Justice of India must make a recommendation to appoint a Judge of the Supreme Court (and to transfer a Chief Justice or puisne Judge of a High Court) in consultation with the four senior-most puisne Judges of the Supreme Court. In so far as an appointment to the High Court is concerned, the recommendation must be made in consultation with the two senior-most puisne Judges of the Supreme Court.

(3) The Chief Justice of India is not entitled to act solely in his individual capacity, without consultation with other Judges of the Supreme Court, in respect of materials and information conveyed by the Government of India for non-appointment of a Judge recommended for appointment.

(4) The view of the other Judges consulted should be in writing and should be conveyed to the Government of India by the Chief Justice of India along with his views to the extent set out in the body of this opinion.

(5) The Chief Justice of India is obliged to comply with the norms and the requirement of the consultation process, as aforestated, in making his recommendations to the Government of India.

(6) Recommendations made by the Chief Justice of India without complying with the norms and requirements of the consultation process, as aforestated, are not binding upon the Government of India.

Another interesting question with respect to appointment of the President of State Commission under the Consumer Protection Act came up for hearing before the Constitution Bench of the Hon'ble Supreme Court in a case reported as *Ashok Tanwar* v. *State of Himachal Pradesh*[1] The Hon'ble Supreme Court held as under:—

> "In the matter of appointing a sitting or retired Judge of a High Court as President of the State Commission process must be initiated by the Chief Justice under section 16 of the Act and 'consultation' contemplated in the said section is 'consultation' only with the Chief Justice of the High Court and not with the collegium. Insistence on 'consultation' by the Chief Justice of a High Court with his two senior-most colleagues in the High Court for the purpose of section 16 of the Act is unwarranted"

The Supreme Court has therefore, held that the consultation as required under section 16 of the Consumer Protection Act cannot be equated to 'consultation' process as required under article 217 of the Constitution of India in relation to appointment of Judge of High Court.

However, there has been an upcry against the system of appointment of High Court and Supreme Court of India Judge and it is suggested that a High Power Judicial Commission be constituted to make the appointment of the judges so that suitable appointment of judges to the superior courts may be made out of the existing talents from the judiciary as well as the Bar.

---

1. AIR 2005 SC 614.

Here reference may be made to the provisions of the Constitution (Amendment) Bill, 1996, which provides for creation of a National Judicial Commission. The Statement of Objects and Reasons, *inter alia*, provides that:

> "The Government of India had announced their intention to set up a High Level Judicial Commission to be called the National Judicial Commission for the appointment of judges of the Supreme Court and of the High Courts and the transfer of judges of the High Courts so as to obviate the criticisms of arbitrariness on the part of the executive in such appointments and transfers and also to make such appointments without any delay. The Law Commission of India in their One Hundred and Twenty-first Report has also emphasised the need for a change in the system. The National Judicial Commission to make recommendation with respect to the appointment of judges of the Supreme Court will consist of the Chief Justice of India and two other judges of the Supreme Court next in seniority to the Chief Justice of India, the Union Minister of Law and Justice, and a senior member of Parliament to be nominated by the Speaker of Lok Sabha. The Commission to make recommendations with respect to the appointment of the judges of the High Courts will consist of the Chief Justice of India, one senior-most Judge of the Supreme Court, the Chief Minister of the State concerned, the Chief Justice of the concerned High Court and one senior-most judge of that High Court."

It is only when competent and independent persons are appointed to the judiciary that the independence of judiciary can be guaranteed. The process of selection of judges should be such that it should inspire confidence in the people. It is, therefore, of utmost importance that great care should be taken in the selection of judges, more so in the case of higher judicial appointments.

REVIEW OF SUPREME COURT ORDERS*

The scope of review of judgments of the courts is extremely limited and the exercise of the power of review is rare. It is only in extreme cases where a review of a Supreme Court judgment can be made and that too within the scope of Order 47 of the Civil Procedure Code. The power of review vested in the Supreme Court is also circumscribed by Order 40, rule 1 of the Supreme Court Rules. The power, however, has to be seen in the context of article 137 and article 145 of the Constitution of India.

A question of the scope of the power of review of the order made by the Supreme Court arose in a recent decision of the Supreme Court reported in Judgements Today *M. Shankaraiah* v. *State of Karnataka*[1], decided on 26-8-1993 by a Bench consisting of S. Ratnavel Pandian, R.M. Sahai & B.P. Jeevan Reddy, JJ. The majority judgment was delivered by Justice R.M. Sahai for himself and on behalf of S. Ratnavel Pandian, J. The Court underlined the role of justice which was paramount and which transcends the role of procedure and the technicalities of law. This is what the Supreme Court held:

> "Justice is a virtue which transcends all barriers. Neither the rules of procedure nor technicalities of law can stand in its way. The order of the Court should not be prejudicial to anyone. Rule of *stare decisis* is adhered to for consistency but it is not as inflexible in Administrative Law as in Public Law. Even the law bends before justice. Entire concept of writ jurisdiction exercised by the higher courts is founded on equity and fairness. If the Court finds that the order was passed under a mistake and it would not have exercised the jurisdiction but for the erroneous assumption which in fact did not exist and it's perpetration shall result in miscarriage of justice then it cannot on any principle be precluded from rectifying the error. Mistake is accepted as valid reason to recall an order. The difference lies in the nature of the mistake and the scope of rectification, depending on if it is of fact or law. But the root from which the power flows is the anxiety to avoid injustice. It is either statutory or inherent. This latter is available where the mistake is of

* First published in The Indian Advocate, Vol. XXV, 1993, p. 72.

1. JT 1993 (5) SC 28.

> the Court. In Administrative Law the scope is still wider. Technicalities apart, if the Court is satisfied of the injustice then it is it's constitutional and legal obligation to set it right by recalling it's order."

In the instant case the Supreme Court was of the view that the earlier Bench did commit an error in placing stipendiary graduates in the scale of first division assistants due to failure to bring correct facts on record. The Supreme Court by the above majority judgment decided that the same could not stand in the way of the Court correcting its mistake and such inequitable consequences that have surfaced now due to a vague affidavit filed by the State cannot be permitted to continue. The Supreme Court further examined the meaning and the scope of the word review as follows:

> "Review literally and even judicially means re-examination or re-consideration. Basic philosophy inherent in it is the universal acceptance of human fallibility. Yet in the realm of law the courts and even the statutes lean strongly in favour of finality of decision legally and properly made. Exceptions both statutorily and judicially have been carved out to correct accidental mistakes or miscarriage of justice. Even when there was no statutory provision and no rules were framed by the highest Court indicating the circumstances in which it could rectify its order the courts culled out such power to avoid abuse of the process or mis-carriage of justice".

The Court relied on the decisions in the case of *Raja Prithvi Chand Lal Choudhury* v. *Sukhraj Rai*[1] The Court also approved the principles laid down by the Privy Council in the case of *Rajinder Narain Rae* v. *Bijai Govind Singh.*[2] By a majority judgment, therefore, the Court allowed the application filed by the State Government and reviewed its earlier orders.

This is a landmark judgment which re-emphasises that justice cannot be made a casualty by the rules of procedure or even the technicalities of law.

In a later judgment of the Supreme Court, a question was raised whether the writ petition is maintainable under article 32 of the Constitution, against the final judgment/order of the Supreme Court after the disposal of a review petition. The case is reported in *Rupa Ashok Hurra* v. *Ashok Hurra.*[3]

The Supreme Court pointed out that article 32 can be invoked only for the purpose of enforcing the fundamental rights conferred in Part II and it is a settled position in law that no judicial order passed by any superior

1. AIR 1941 FC 1.
2. I Moo PC 117.
3. AIR 2002 SC 177.

Court in judicial proceedings can be said to violate any of the fundamental rights enshrined in Part III. It may further be noted that the superior Courts of justice do not also fall within the ambit of State or other authorities under article 12 of the Constitution.

The Constitution Bench of the Supreme Court considered the various earlier decisions of the Supreme Court including the decisions in the case of *A.R. Antulay* v. *R.S. Naik.*[1] Ultimately the Supreme Court held as under:—

> "On the analysis of the ratio laid down in the aforementioned cases we affirm our considered view that a final judgment/order passed by this Court cannot be assailed in an application under article 32 of the Constitution of India by an aggrieved person whether he was a party to the case or not".

However, the Hon'ble Supreme Court further held as under:

> "We are of the view that though Judges of the highest Court do their best, subject of course to the limitation of human fallibility, yet situations may arise, in the rarest of rare cases, which would require reconsideration of a final judgment to set right miscarriage of justice complained of. In such case it would not only be proper but also obligatory both legally and morally to rectify the error. After giving our anxious consideration to the question we are persuaded to hold that the duty to do justice in these rarest of rare cases shall have to prevail over the policy of certainty of judgment as though it is essentially in public interest that a final judgment of the final Court in the country should not be open to challenge yet there may be circumstances, as mentioned above, wherein declining to reconsider the judgment would be oppressive to judicial conscience and cause perpetuation of irremediable injustice".

It will be thus seen that the Hon'ble Supreme Court has always considered the right of a person to secure justice as of paramount importance and preserved the right of the Supreme Court to set right any miscarriage of justice occasioned by any judgment of the Supreme Court.

Appearance in Person Before the Supreme Court

The question of personal appearance of persons before the courts to argue their own cases has assumed significance in recent times. The number of persons wishing to argue their own cases in the courts and even in the Apex Court is on the rise.

A question of this nature arose before the Supreme Court in the case of *Bhubaneshwar Singh* v. *Union of India*[2], decided on 1-9-1993. The case

1. AIR (1998) 2 SCC 602.
2. JT 1993 (5) SC 154.

was heard by a Bench consisting of J.S. Verma and Dr. A.S. Anand, JJ. The Appellant in this case appeared in person and made a submission in Hindi, not being familiar with the Court language. The Court suggested to him that it could provide him the assistance of an Advocate through the Legal Aid Board or request one of the Advocates to appear for him as *amicus curiae* without any financial burden on him. The Appellant did not want the assistance of any counsel and insisted on arguing the matter himself. Although the Court repeatedly advised him to argue only on relevant issues, he insisted on arguing at length and a lot of judicial time was taken up. The Court did not appreciate this attitude and this is what the Court had to say about such matters:

> "Taking note of the increase in the number of cases in which the parties appear in person in this Court, we feel that a stage has now reached when this Court, on the administrative side, is required to consider the desirability of providing some procedure to scrutinise their petitions and screen the parties, appearing in person, and only such of the parties who are certified by an authority/committee as "competent" to assist the Court in person, may, with the leave of the Court, be permitted to argue in person. Those of the litigants, who are not so certified, or those to whom leave is not granted by the Court, should be referred to the Legal Aid and Advice Board or the "Supreme Court Senior Advocates Free Legal Aid Society", which is a voluntary body and offers assistance, in appropriate cases, irrespective of the financial position of the concerned litigant. Apart from providing proper assistance to the Court, the assistance by the lawyers would ultimately tend to be in the interest of the litigants themselves. It would also take care of preventing objectionable and unparliamentary language in the pleadings, which some of the 'parties in person' permit themselves the liberty of indulging in, not being familiar with the court craft and the bounds of law within which the parties must formulate their pleadings in proper language. Such a course would advance public interest while safeguarding individual interest also."

The Court also appreciated the role of lawyers in giving assistance to the Court and this is what the Court said:

> "Our experience shows that every advocate, senior, not so senior and junior, whenever requested by the Court to offer assistance has responded positively and generously and therefore the interest of the 'party in person' who would be represented by such a counsel would stand adequately protected."

CONTROL OF SUBORDINATE JUDICIARY BY THE HIGH COURTS

In a recent, landmark judgment of a Supreme Court Bench (Dr. A.S. Anand, S.P. Bharucha and B.N. Kirpal, JJ), the important question of law regarding the powers of the High Court, to make an enquiry against the officers of the subordinate judiciary, under article 235 of the Constitution of India came up for hearing. The petitioner in this case was a member of the Rajasthan Higher Judicial Service and filed a petition under article 32 of the Constitution of India assailing the disciplinary proceedings which had been initiated against him pursuant to a Full Bench resolution of the Rajasthan High Court.

The first submission made by the petitioner was that after the passing of an order by the Chief Justice, the complaint of one Vijay Singh stood disposed off, and it could not be reopened by the full Court or the then Chief Justice specially when there was no attenuating circumstances by way of fresh evidence or material which would warrant a fresh look in the matter and there was no such fresh material.

The second submission was that the initiation of the disciplinary proceedings by issuing a charge-sheet levelling charges which were stale and on materials gathered as an afterthought was an action tainted with malice and such proceedings were liable to be quashed as being *mala fide* and being malicious in law.

Article 235 of the Constitution of India deals with the control of the High Court over subordinate courts and reads as under:

> "**235. Control over subordinate courts.**—Control over district courts and courts subordinate thereto including the posting and promotion of, and the grant of leave to persons belonging to the judicial service of a State and holding any post inferior to the post of District Judge shall be vested in the High Court, but nothing in this article shall be construed as taking away from any such person any right of appeal which he may have under the law regulating the conditions of his service or as authorising the High Court to deal

with him otherwise than in accordance with the conditions of his service prescribed under such law."

The Hon'ble Supreme Court examined the relevant rules *viz* rules 14, 15 and 32 of Chapter III of the Rajasthan High Court Rules, 1952, which deal with the conduct of the administrative business of the court, The Hon'ble Supreme Court held that every complaint received against a judicial officer is not required to be brought before the full Court unless and until the question of removal or dismissal of the judicial officer arises. The Supreme Court held that it was competent for the Chief Justice specially in view of the provision of sub-rule (2) of rule 32, while dealing with the complaint received against petitioner to decide that no action thereon was called for and therefore there was no illegality or impropriety committed by the Chief Justice when he decided that the complaint did not call for any disciplinary action against the petitioner. The Hon'ble members of the full Court when they passed the impugned resolution, there was no valid reason in law for the full Court to revoke the decision taken by the then Chief Justice.

On the second submission made by the petitioner the Hon'ble Supreme Court held that there was a complete lack of *bona fide* on the part of the High Court when it decided to institute disciplinary proceedings against the petitioner, after the earlier Chief Justice had already held that no decision was required to be taken on the said complaint against the petitioner.

The Supreme Court significantly also made observation regarding the protection required for the independent functioning of the subordinate Courts. The Court adversely commented on the full Court in the following manner:—

> "This case leaves us very sad. Entrustment of the control of the subordinate judiciary to the High Courts by enactment of the relevant provisions in the Constitution of India, particularly article 235 therein is for the purpose of ensuring their independence and protection from executive interference. At a time when fairness and non-arbitrariness are the essential requirements of every administrative state action, it is more so for any administrative act of the Judges. It is necessary that members of the subordinate judiciary get no occasion to think otherwise. We are afraid, this incident appears to shake this faith. We do hope it is an inadvertent exception."

In this view of the matter, the Court allowed the writ petition and quashed the entire disciplinary proceedings initiated by the High Court against the petitioner together with the full Court resolution and the High

Court of Rajasthan was directed to pay exemplary cost of Rs. 20,000 to the petitioner.

This is a landmark judgment of the Supreme Court dealing with the powers of the High Court to control the subordinate judiciary, and to ensure the independence and protection of the subordinate judiciary, which is equally important for administration of justice.

CONSTITUTION OF TRIBUNALS—IS CONSULTATION WITH CHIEF JUSTICE OF HIGH COURT NECESSARY?

The question whether a Tribunal constituted with composition of judicial and administrative members by the Government, would be justified and constitutionally valid when there is no consultation with the Chief Justice of the High Court in their appointment came up for consideration before the Bench of the Supreme Court consisting of Sujata V. Manohar & S. Rajendra Babu, JJ. The Bench in a landmark judgment reported as JT 1998 (4) SC 110 decided that such Tribunal does not become unconstitutional merely because there is no consultation with the Chief Justice of the High Court. The proceeding arose out of the writ petition filed before the Andhra Pradesh High Court challenging the constitutional validity of the Andhra Pradesh Land Grabbing (Prohibition) Act, 1982. The Andhra Pradesh High Court had given *inter alia* directions restraining the State of Andhra Pradesh from making any appointment of judicial member and revenue member without the consultation in respect of the selection of such member/members with the Chief Justice of the High Court. Section 7 of the said Act provided for Constitution of a Special Court and *inter alia* the following qualifications were laid down for the appointment of the Chairman and of the other members of the Tribunal:—

> "The Chairman shall be a person who is or has been a judge of a High Court and of the other four members, two shall be persons who are or have been District Judges (hereinafter referred to as judicial members) and the other two members shall be persons who hold or have held the post not below the rank of a District Collector (hereinafter referred to as revenue members)".

In view of article 323(B) of the Constitution of India, the Supreme Court held that the Act which sets up Special Court for land grabbing cases is within the legislative competence of the State Government. It was contended by the petitioner that in the case of other members of the Tribunal, that is to say two persons who are or have been District Judges and two persons who hold or have held a post not below the rank of a District Collector, there was no provision for consultation with the Chief Justice of the High Court concerned, and therefore, the constitution of such Tribunal was unconstitutional. It was contended that a member of the Tribunal constituted under article 323(B) of the Constitution must enjoy the same degree of independence and freedom from executive influence as is enjoyed by the higher judiciary, and if there is no consultation with the Chief Justice of the High Court in the appointments to the Special Court or Tribunal, this independence will be affected:

> "Obviously, therefore, if the Administrative Tribunal is created in substitution of the High Court and the jurisdiction of the High Court under articles 226 and 227 is taken away and vested in the Administrative Tribunal, the same independence from possibility of executive pressure or influence must also be ensured to the Chairman, Vice-Chairman and Members of the Administrative Tribunal, or else the Administrative Tribunal would cease to be an equally effective and efficacious substitute for the High Court and provisions of the impugned Act would be rendered invalid."

Reliance was placed on the observations made in *S.P. Sampat Kumar* v. *Union of India.*[1]

However, the Bench of the Supreme Court held that in view of subsequent decisions of the Supreme Court in *L. Chandra Kumar* v. *Union of India,*[2] wherein the Court had held that the power of judicial review vested in the High Courts under articles 226 and 227 and in the Supreme Court under article 32 of the Constitution, is an integral and essential feature of the Constitution constituting a part of its basic structure. Therefore, the power of judicial review cannot be ousted or excluded.

In view of this judgment, it was held by the Bench that observations in the case of *S.P. Sampat Kumar* will not apply. The Bench held as under:—

> "In the perspective of these observations it would not be correct to hold that because the Members of the Special Court, in the present cases, can be appointed by the Government without consulting the Chief Justice of the State, the Special Court is an unconstitutional Court, since its members do not enjoy the same degree of independence as the members of the higher judiciary, especially when the Chairman's appointment is in consultation with the Chief Justice of the State. Also, the remedy under articles 226 and 227 is available against the orders of the Special Court".

---

1. (1987) 1 SCC 124.
2. (1997) 3 SCC 261.

The Supreme Court, therefore, held that the High Court, had erred in giving directions for mandatory consultation with the Chief Justice of the High Court in the case of appointment of all members including revenue members of the special Court and the High Court was also not right in directing that existing appointment made to the special court should be placed before it for opinion of the Chief Justice of the High Court and consequently the judgment was set aside. This is an important judgment of the Supreme Court, which reiterates that judicial power vested in the High Court under articles 226 and 227 and in the Supreme Court under article 32 of the Constitution of India is an integral and essential feature of the Constitution, constituting a part of its basic structure. However, the power of the State Government to make appointments of members of the Tribunals under article 323B of the Constitution has been upheld.

Part III

Law and Society

LAW AND SOCIETY

SHOULD THE DEATH PENALTY BE ABOLISHED?

Recently, the judgments in the *Naina Sahni and Priya Darshine Mattoo's* cases in relation to awarding death penalty have been in the news. In the news the most prominent case is that of death penalty awarded to terrorist Afzal who was responsible for the most heinous attack on Parliament and whose mercy petition is pending before the President of India along with many others. These cases have again revived the question about the necessity or otherwise of the retention of the death penalty under the provisions of the Indian Penal Code. The legality of the imposition of death sentence has been the subject-matter of many decisions of the Supreme Court. It would be advisable to refer to the decisions of the Supreme Court, including the decisions of the Constitutional Benches of the Supreme Court, in this connection.

In *Jagmohan Singh* v. *State of Uttar Pradesh*[1], the imposition of death sentence was challenged before the Bench of Mr. Justice S.M. Sikri. C.J., A.N. Ray, I.D. Dua, D.G. Palekar and M.H. Beg, JJ. It was held in the case that the provisions of section 302 imposing death sentences are not violative of article 14 of the Constitution on the grounds that unguided and uncontrolled discretion is given to Judges to impose capital punishment or imprisonment for life. It was also held that even assuming that the right to live is basic to the freedoms mentioned under article 19, it cannot be held that the capital punishment as such is unreasonable or not required in the public interest.

Reliance was also placed by the Judges on the Law Commission of India's 35th report published in 1967 and particularly to the following observations:

> "Having regard, however, to the conditions of India, to the variety of the social upbringing of its inhabitants, to the disparity in the level of morality and education in the country, to the vastness of its area, to the diversity of its population and to the paramount need for maintaining law and order in the country at the present juncture, India cannot risk the experiment of abolition of capital punishment.

1. AIR 1973 SC 947.

On a consideration of all the issues the Law Commission was of the opinion that the capital punishment should be retained in the present state of the country". The matter was again agitated before a Bench of the Hon'ble Supreme Court in the case of *Bachan Singh* v. *State of Punjab* comprising Mr. Justice Y.V. Chandrachud, C.J., P.N. Bhagwati, R.S. Sarkaria, A.C. Gupta and N.L. Untwalia, JJ. The majority judgment excepting that of Mr. Justice Bhagwati was reported in the AIR 1980 SC 898. It was held that the provisions of death penalty as an alternate punishment for murder under section 302 of the Indian Penal Code is not unreasonable and it is in the public interest and therefore it cannot be held that the impugned provisions in section 302 violates either the letter or the ethos of article 19 of the Constitution. It was also held that the provisions of death penalty as an alternate arrangement for murder is not violative of article 21 of the Constitution of India.

Reliance was again placed on the 35th Report of the Law Commission of India, which it had made after an intensive and extensive study of the subject of death penalty in India. Following arguments of the abolitionists which had been substantially adopted by the Counsel for the petitioner were noted as under:—

"(a) The death penalty is irreversible. Decided upon accordingly to fallible processes of law by fallible human beings, it can be – and actually has been – inflicted upon people innocent of any crime.

(b) There is no convincing evidence to show that death penalty serves any penological purpose:—

(i) Its deterrent effect remains unproven. It has not been shown that incidence of murder has increased in countries where death penalty has been abolished, after its abolition.

(ii) Retribution in the sense of vengeance is no longer an acceptable end of punishment.

(iii) On the contrary, reformation of the criminal and his rehabilitation is the primary purpose of punishment. Imposition of death penalty nullifies that purpose.

(c) Execution by whatever means and for whatever offence is a cruel, inhuman and degrading punishment."

But the same were rejected and not found acceptable by the judges (except Mr. Justice P.N. Bhagwati, who delivered a separate judgment). Reliance was also placed by the Court on its earlier decision in *Jagmohan's* case.[1]

---

1. AIR 1973 SC 947.

In accordance with the majority opinion the challenge to the constitutionality of section 302 of the Penal Code insofar as it provides for the death sentence as also the challenge to the constitutionality of section 354(3) of the Code of Criminal Procedure, 1973 failed and was rejected.

Validity of the death sentence was again challenged in the year 1992 in the case of *Shashi Nayar* v. *Union of India*[1], which was heard and decided by K.N. Singh, P.B. Sawant, N.M. Kasliwal, B.P. Jeevan Reddy and G.N. Ray, JJ. Reliance was again placed on the earlier decision in the case of *Shri Jagmohan* and the majority judgment in *Bachan Singh's* case. It was held as under:

> "The majority opinion in *Bachan Singh's* case held that having regard to the social conditions in our country the stage was not ripe for taking a risk of abolishing it. No material has been placed before us to show that the view taken in *Bachan Singh's* case requires reconsideration. Further, a judicial notice can be taken of the fact that the law and order situation in the country has not only improved since 1967 but has deteriorated over the years and it is fast worsening today. The present is therefore the most inopportune time to reconsider the law on the subject. Hence, the request for referring the matter to a larger Bench is rejected".

Reference may be made to few of the cases of the Supreme Court involving imposition of death sentences, where the Hon'ble Supreme Court has awarded the death sentence. Reference may be made to a case reported in *Sk. Ishaque* v. *State of Bihar*.[2] The Supreme Court held as under:—

> "The imposition of proper sentence is an obligation on the court and even if no argument had been addressed on behalf of the appellants, the court was expected to take note of the legislative intendment relating to the award of capital punishment as manifest from the provisions of section 354(3) Cr. P.C. and award an appropriate sentence, after taking into account the aggravating as well as the mitigating circumstances. The sentencing court has to make an endeavour to see that all relevant factors and circumstances bearing on the question of sentence , are taken note of and only after giving due weight to the same, it should proceed to impose the capital sentence. An eye for an eye approach is neither proper nor desirable. The mandate of section 354(3) Cr. P.C. does not approve of it. The courts must be conscious of the change brought about in the matter of award of capital punishment by the legislature by

1. AIR 1992 SC 395.
2. (1995) 3 SCC 392.

> enacting section 354(3) Cr. P.C. limiting the award the sentence of death only in the "rarest of the rare cases" and that too after recording "special reasons" for awarding the same".

The Supreme Court referred to its earlier decisions in *Bachan Singh* v. *State of Punjab*[1] and *Anshad* v. *State of Karnataka*.[2] In an another case *Holiram Bordoloi* v. *State of Assam*[3], the Supreme Court held that the following circumstances were the aggravating circumstances for the imposition of capital punishment:—

> "In the present case the aggravating circumstances against the accused are (a) this is a case of cold-blooded murder; (b) the accused was leading the gang; (c) The victims did not provoke or contribute to the incident; (d) two victims were burnt to death by locking the house from outside; (e) one of the victims was a young boy, aged about 6 years, who, somehow, managed to come out of the burning house, but he was mercilessly thrown back to the fire by the appellant; (f) the dragging of *Nagarmol Bordoloi* by the appellant *Holiram* to his house and then cutting him into pieces in broad day-light in the presence of bystanders; (g) the entire incident took place in the broad day-light and the crime was committed in the most barbaric manner to deter others from challenging the supremacy of the appellant in the village; (h) the entire incident was preplanned by the accused-appellant *Holiram*". Under these circumstances the Supreme Court held that there were no mitigating circumstances to refrain from imposing the death penalty on the appellant. The Supreme Court in another case *Saibanna* v. *State of Karnataka*[4], the Hon'ble Supreme Court referred to the following circumstances enumerated by the High Court as indicative that it is one of the "rarest of rare case" where imposition of death penalty is justified:—
>
> (1) The accused was already convicted to life imprisonment for murder of his first wife Malakawwa. He committed the present murders while he was out on parole.
>
> (2) That the murder was the result of pre-planning on his part is evident from the fact that the murder weapon is a *jambia*, a hunting knife used for attack, not ordinarily available in a house.
>
> (3) Even if the accused had some reason to suspect the fidelity of his wife, which motivated him to murder her, there could have

1. (1980) 2 SCC 684.
2. (1994) 4 SCC 381.
3. AIR 2005 SC 2059.
4. (2005) 4 SCC 165.

been absolutely no reason for killing the defenceless child of 1½ years of age.

(4) The murders were committed when the victims were helpless and asleep.

(5) No extenuating circumstances in favour of the accused were either pleaded or proved.

The Supreme Court taking into account all the circumstances held that the High Court was right in coming to the conclusion that the appellant's case bristles with special circumstances requisite for imposition of the death sentence.

It would also be appropriate to know the position of other countries of the world, regarding the imposition of death sentence. According to the Report in the Times of India under the heading "400 waiting in death row" as given below:—

> "As of now, as many as 129 countries have abolished it in law or in practice, while 68 countries still retain it, among them 38 States of the US, Japan, Cuba, Egypt, China, Saudi Arabia, Pakistan and, of course India".

In a book by Dr. Janak Raj Jai, Advocate, Supreme Court of India on Death Penalty, the author has relied on the views of Justice Krishna Iyer and Justice P.N. Bhagwati (former Judges of the Supreme Court), in favour of abolition of death penalty, and which are supported by the views of some eminent lawyers including Mr. P.P. Rao, Senior Advocate and Justice Rajender Sachar, Former Chief Justice, Delhi High Court. Various other professors of law and eminent lawyers have all supported the abolition of the death sentence.

However, I am not in agreement with this view, howsoever laudable it may appear to be.

I am in respectful agreement with the view that the law and order situation in the country is worsening today and therefore, it is not the right time to abolish death penalty. Cases involving terrorists attack on Akshardham Temple, attack on the Parliament House and terrorists attack in the Jammu and Kashmir area are a pointer in this direction. Death penalty alone can provide some kind of deterrence in cases involving sovereignty and integrity of the country.

Even otherwise cases relating to robbery, rape, abduction, extortion, etc. leading to murder have increased manifold during the recent times and death penalty is the only penalty that can provide some kind of deterrence in such cases.

RIGHT TO DIE *QUA* ARTICLE 21*

The important question regarding the scope of section 309 of the Indian Penal Code which makes an attempt to suicide punishable offence arose before the Supreme Court of India, in a very recent case reported in *P. Rathinam Nagbhusan Patnaik* v. *Union of India*.[1] The Hon'ble Division Bench of the Supreme Court in a landmark judgment held that section 309 was violative of article 21 of the Constitution of India and declared it as void. The judgment deals with the various aspects *viz.*, religious, moral and legal, of suicide and has made a comparative study of the laws in various parts of the world. It is in this context that the Division Bench deals with the scope of article 21 of the Constitution of India *qua* the right of a person residing in India claiming a right to die within its compass. The Supreme Court referred to its earlier decision in *Unnikrishnan* v. *State of Andhra Pradesh*[2], wherein reference has been made about the various rights which had been held to be covered under article 21. These being:

1. The right to go abroad; *Satwant Singh Sawhney* v. *D. Ramarathnam APO, New Delhi*.[3]
2. The right to privacy; *Govind* v. *State of Madhya Pradesh*.[4] In this case reliance was placed on the American decision in *Griwsold* v. *Connecticut*.[5]
3. The right against solitary confinement; *Sunil Batra* v. *Delhi Administration*.[6]
4. The right against the fetters; *Charles Shobraj* v. *Supdt. Central Jail*.[7]
5. The right to legal aid; *M.H. Hoaskot* v. *State of Maharashtra*.[8]

---

* The judgment of the Supreme Court referred to in the above Article *viz. P. Rathinam Nagbhusan Patnaik* v. *Union of India*, JT 1994 (3) SC 392 has been overruled in the judgment of the Supreme Court reported in AIR 1996 SC 1257 decided by Bench of 5 Judges and wherein it has been held that "right to die", if any, is inherently inconsistent with the 'right to life' as is 'death with life'. It was also held in the said judgment that neither of the provisions *viz.* (Sections 306 & 309), IPC is constitutionally invalid.

1. JT 1994 (3) SC 392.
2. (1993) 1 SCC 645.
3. AIR 1967 SC 1836.
4. 1975 Cr LJ 1111: AIR 1975 SC 1378.
5. (1965) 381 US 479.
6. AIR 1978 SC 1675: (1978) Cr LJ 1741.
7. AIR 1978 SC 1514: 1978 Cri LJ 1534.
8. AIR 1978 SC 1548: (1978) Cr LJ 1678: (1979) 1 SCR 192.

6. The right to speedy trial; *Hussainara Khatoon* v. *Home Secretary, State of Bihar.*[1]
7. The right against handcuffing; *Prem Shankar Shukla* v. *Delhi Administration.*[2]
8. The right against delayed execution; *T.V. Vatheeswaran* v. *State of Tamil Nadu.*[3]
9. The right against custodial violence; *Sheela Barse* v. *State of Maharashtra.*[4]
10. The right against public hanging; *A.G. of India* v. *Lachma Devi.*[5]
11. Doctor's assistance; *Parmanand Katara* v. *Union of India.*[6]
12. Shelter; *Shantistar Builders* v. *N.K. Totame.*[7]

Reference was also made to the judgment of Field, J. in *Munn* v. *Illinois,*[8] in which it was held that the term life (as appearing in the 5th and 14th amendments to the Constitution of United States) means something more than merely animal existence. This view had been accepted in various judgments of the Supreme Court wherein it has been held that the word "LIFE" in article 21 means:

> "Right to live with human dignity and the same does not merely connote continued drudgery. It takes within its fold 'some of the finer graces of human civilisation which makes life worth living', and that the expanded concept of life would mean the 'tradition, culture and heritage' of the concerned person."

If a person has a right to live, question arises whether he also has a right not to live. Reference may be made to decision of the Supreme Court in *R.C. Cooper* v. *Union of India,*[9] wherein it was stated that it cannot be seriously disputed that fundamental rights have their positive as well as their negative aspects, for example:

> "Freedom of speech and expression includes freedom not to speak. Similarly, the freedom of association and movement includes freedom not to join any association or move anywhere. So too, freedom of business includes freedom not to do business. It was, therefore, stated that logically it must follow that the right to live will include right not to live, *i.e.* right to die or to terminate one's life."

---

1. AIR 1979 SC 1360: (1979) Cr LJ 1036: (1979) 3 SCR 169.
2. AIR 1980 SC 1535: (1980) Cr LJ 930: (1980) 3 SCC 526.
3. AIR 1983 SC 361: (1983) Cr LJ 481.
4. AIR 1983 SC 378: (1983) Cr LJ 642.
5. AIR 1986 SC 467: (1986) Cr LJ 364.
6. AIR 1989 SC 2039: (1990) Cr LJ 671.
7. AIR 1990 SC 630.
8. 1876 (94) US 113.
9. AIR 1970 SC 1318.

Keeping in view various judgments of the American Courts and the Indian Courts it was held that the right to live which article 21 speaks of can be to bring in its trail the right not to live a forced life.

However, in a later case reported as *Gian Kaur* v. *State of Punjab,*[1] which came up for hearing before the Constitution Bench of 5 Judges, the Hon'ble Supreme Court reversed its earlier decision and held that the right to life does not include the right to die. The Supreme Court analysed the various earlier decisions *viz. P. Rathinam* v. *Union of India,*[2] the Supreme Court held as under:—

> To give meaning and content to the word 'life' in article 21, it has been construed as life with human dignity. Any aspect of life which makes it dignified may be read into it but not that which extinguishes it and is, therefore, inconsistent with the continued existence of life resulting in effacing the right itself. The 'right to die', if any, is inherently inconsistent with the 'right to life' as is 'death with life'.

In view of this matter, the Supreme Court, therefore, held that "the question of constitutional validity of sections 306 and 309, I.P.C. are decided accordingly, by holding the neither of the two provisions is constitutionally invalid".

In another case reported as *Banwari Lal Sharma (Dr.)* v. *State of Punjab.*[3] The decision of the Supreme Court in *Gian Kaur* v. *State of Punjab*[4] was followed. Relying on the Constitution Bench of the Supreme Court in *Gian Kaur* v. *State of Punjab,*[4] the Writ Petition was dismissed.

The judgment of the Supreme Court dealt with myriad aspects of the causes and effects of suicide. However, the question whether the right to die is included within the scope and meaning of article 21 of the Constitution of India, is of paramount importance.

---

1. AIR 1996 SC 946.
2. 1994 AIR SCW 1764: (1994) 3 SCC 394: AIR 1994 SC 1844.
3. (1998) 3 SCC 604.
4. (1996) 2 SCC 648.

MEDICAL PRACTITIONERS AND THE CONSUMER PROTECTION ACT*

An important landmark judgment of the Supreme Court reported as (*Indian Medical Association* v. *V.P. Shantha*,[1] decided on 13-11-1995) deals with the following significant questions:

1. Whether and, if so in what circumstances a medical practitioner can be regarded as rendering 'service' under section 2(1)(o) of the Consumer Protection Act, 1986 (the Act).
2. Whether the service rendered at hospital/nursing home can be regarded as 'service' under section 2(1)(o) of the Act. These questions have been earlier considered by various High Courts as well as by the National Consumer Disputes Redressal Commission (the National Commission).

   There were conflicting judgments of the various courts on these issues. In *A.S. Chandra (Dr.)* v. *Union of India*,[2] a Division Bench of Andhra Pradesh High Court held that service rendered for consideration by private medical practitioners, private hospitals and nursing homes must be construed as 'service' for the purpose of section 2(1)(o) of the Act and the persons availing such service are 'Consumers' within the meaning of section 2(1)(d) of the Act.

In *C.S. Subramanian (Dr.)* v. *Kumarasamy*,[3] a Division Bench of the Madras High Court had, however, taken a different view. It had been

* The liability of Doctors for death caused by rashness/negligence has been decided by the Supreme Court in the judgment of *Jacob Mathew (Dr.)* v. *State of Punjab*, decided on 5-8-2005 and reported in 122 (2005) DLT 83 (SC) wherein 8 principles of laws have been laid down. *Inter alia* it has been held that a simple lack of care, error of judgment or accident is not a proof of negligence on the part of the medical professional.

Similarly in a case reported in the case of *Suresh Gupta (Dr.)* decided by the Bench of two Judges *vide* their judgment dated 4-8-2004, it has been held that no case of recklessness or gross negligence had been made out against the doctor to compel him to face trial under section 304(a) of the I.P.C. The appeal was allowed and the order of the Magistrate and the High Court was set aside and the criminal proceedings pending against the doctor were quashed.

1. JT 1995 (8) SC 119.
2. (1992) 1 Andh LT 713.
3. (1994) 1 MLJ 438.

held that the services rendered to a patient by a medical practitioner or by a hospital by way of diagnosis and treatment, both medical and surgical, would not come within the definition of 'service' under section 2(1)(o) of the Act and a patient who undergoes treatment under a medical practitioner or a hospital by way of diagnosis and treatment, both medical and surgical, cannot be considered to be a 'consumer' within the meaning of section 2(1)(d) of the Act; but the medical practitioners or hospitals undertaking and providing para-medical services of all kinds and categories cannot claim similar immunity from the provision of the Act and that they would fall, to the extent of such para-medical service rendered by them, within the definition of 'service' and a person availing of such service would be a 'consumer' within the meaning of the Act.

The National Commission by its judgment and order dated December 15, 1989 in First Appeal No. 2 of 1989 had held that persons who avail themselves of the facility of medical treatment in government hospitals are not 'consumers' and the said facility offered in the government hospitals cannot be regarded as service 'hired' for 'consideration'. It had been held that the payment of direct or indirect taxes by the public does not constitute 'consideration' paid for hiring the services rendered in the government hospitals. It had also been held that contribution made by a government employee in the Central Government Health Scheme or such other similar schemes does not make him a 'consumer' within the meaning of the Act.

By judgment dated April 21, 1992 in First Appeal Nos. 48 and 94 of 1991, the National Commission had held that the activity of providing medical assistance for payment carried on by hospitals and members of the medical profession falls within the scope of the expression 'service' as defined in section 2(1)(o) of the Act and that in the event of any deficiency in the performance of such service, the aggrieved party can invoke the remedies provided under the Act by filing a complaint before the Consumer Forum having jurisdiction.

By judgment dated May 3, 1993, the National Commission had held that since the treatment that was given to the complainant's deceased husband in the nursing home belonging to the opposite party was totally free of charges, it did not constitute 'service' as defined under the Act and the complainant was not entitled to seek any relief under the Act. C.A. No. 254/94 had been filed by the complainant against the said judgment of the National Commission.

Another petition had been filed under article 32 of the Constitution by *Cosmopolitan Hospital (P) Ltd.*, and *Dr. K. Venugopalan Nair* [petitioner in SLP (C) Nos. 6885 and 6950/02] wherein the said petitioners had assailed the validity of the provisions of the Act. Insofar as they were held to be applicable to the medical profession, as being violative of the articles 14 and 19(1)(g) of the Constitution.

The Bench of the Hon'ble Supreme Court comprising of Justice Kuldip Singh, Justice S.C. Aggarwal and Justice B.L. Hansaria after a very thorough and exhaustive consideration laid down the following law in relation to the applicability of the Consumer Protection Act *qua* the medical practitioners:—

1. Service rendered to a patient by medical practitioner (except where the doctor renders service free of charge to every patient or under a contract of personal service), by way of consultation, diagnosis and treatment, both medical and surgical, would fall within the ambit of 'service' as defined in section 2(1)(o) of the Act.
2. The fact that medical practitioners belong to the medical profession and are subject to the disciplinary control of the Medical Council of India and/or State Medical Councils constituted under the provisions of the Indian Medical Council Act would not exclude the services rendered by them from the ambit of the Act.
3. A 'contract of personal service' has to be distinguished from a 'contract for personal service'. In the absence of a relationship of master and servant between the patient and the medical practitioner, the service rendered by a medical practitioner to the patient cannot be regarded as service rendered under a 'contract of personal service'. Such service is service rendered under a 'contract for personal service' and is not covered by exclusionary clause of the definition of 'service' contained in section 2(1)(o) of the Act.
4. The expression 'contract of personal service' in section 2(1)(o) of the Act cannot be confined to contracts of employment of domestic servants only and the said expression would include the employment of a medical officer for the purpose rendering medical service to the employer. The service rendered by a medical officer to his employer under the contract of employment would be outside the purview of 'service' as defined in section 2(1)(o) of the Act.
5. Service rendered free of charge by a medical practitioner attached to a hospital/nursing home or a medical officer employed in a Hospital/Nursing Home where such services are rendered free of charge to everybody, would not be 'service' as defined in section 2(1)(o) of the Act. The payment of a token

amount for registration purpose only at the hospital/nursing home would not alter the position.

6. Service rendered at a non-Government hospital/Nursing home where no charge whatsoever is made from any person availing the service and all patients (rich and poor) are given free service is outside the purview of the expression 'service' as defined in section 2(1)(o) of the Act. The payment of a token amount for registration purpose only at the hospital/Nursing home would not alter the position.
7. Service rendered at a non-Government hospital/Nursing home where charges are required to be paid by the person availing such services falls within the purview of the expression 'service' as defined in section 2(1)(o) of the Act.
8. Service rendered at a non-Government hospital/Nursing home where charges are required to be paid by persons who are in a position to pay and persons who cannot afford to pay are rendered service free of charge would fall within the ambit of expression 'service' as defined in section 2(1)(o) of the Act irrespective of the fact that the service is rendered free of charge to persons who are not in a position to pay for such services. Free service, would also be 'service' and the recipient a 'consumer' under the Act.
9. Service rendered at Government Hospital/Health Centre/ dispensary where no charge whatsoever is made from any person availing the services and all patients (rich and poor) are given free service—is outside the purview of the expression 'service' as defined in section 2(1)(o) of the Act. The payment of a token amount for registration purpose only at the hospital/ Nursing Home would not alter the position.
10. Service rendered at a Government Hospital/Health Centre/ dispensary where services are rendered on payment of charges and also rendered free of charge to other persons availing such service would fall within the ambit of the expression 'service' as defined in section 2(1)(o) of the Act irrespective of the fact that the service is rendered free of charge to persons who do not pay for such service. Free service would also be 'service' and the recipient a 'consumer' under the Act.
11. Service rendered by a medical practitioner or hospital/Nursing home cannot be regarded as service rendered free of charge, if a person availing the service has taken an insurance policy for medical care whereunder the charges for consultation, diagnosis and medical treatment are borne by the Insurance

Company and such service would fall within the ambit of 'service' as defined in section 2(1)(o) of the Act.

12. Similarly, where, as a part of the conditions of service, the employer bears the expenses of medical treatment of an employee or his family members dependent on him, the service rendered to such an employee and his family members by a medical practitioner or a hospital/Nursing home would not be free of charge and would constitute 'service' under section 2(1)(o) of the Act.

This decision is a monumental decision and covers the entire field of practice of medical practitioners irrespective of whether they are working full-time or part-time in Government hospitals and/or other private clinics, or are working privately alone. The judgment, however, may also lead to cases of other professionals and whether they would also be covered under the Consumer Protection Act, 1986, the decision in any case would have far and wide ramifications.

In the case *Spring Meadows Hospital* v. *Harjot Ahluwalia*,[1] the Supreme Court held as under:—

"Gross medical mistake will always result in a finding of negligence. Use of wrong drug or wrong gas during the course of anaesthetic will frequently lead to the imposition of liability and in some situations even the principle of *res ipsa loquitur* can be applied. Even delegation of responsibility to another may amount to negligence in certain circumstances. A consultant could be negligent where he delegates the responsibility to his junior with the knowledge that the junior was incapable of performing his duties properly".

With regard to the scope of clause (ii) section 2(1) (d), the Supreme Court held as under:—

"The definition clause being wide enough to include not only the person who hires the services but also the beneficiary of such services which beneficiary to other than the person who hires the services, the conclusion is irresistible that both the parents of the child as well as the child would be consumer within the meaning of section 2(1)(d)(ii) of the Act and as such can claim compensation under the Act".

In an another case *State of Haryana* v. *Santra*.[2] The Supreme Court also referred its earlier decisions reported in *Poonam Verma* v. *Ashwin Patel*[3]

1. AIR 1998 SC 1806.
2. AIR 2000 SC 1888.
3. AIR 1996 SC 2111.

and *Spring Meadows Hospital* v. *Harjot Ahluwalia*[1] The Supreme Court with the approval of the verdict of the judgment of the House of Lords in *Whitehouse* v. *Jordan*,[2] held as under:—

> "The true position is that an error of judgment may, or may not, be negligent: it depends on the nature of the error. If it is one that would not have been made by a reasonably competent professional man professing to have the standard and type of skill that the defendant holds himself out as having, and acting with ordinary care, then it is negligence. If, on the other hand, it is an error that such a man, acting with ordinary care, might have made, then it is not negligence". Having regard to the authorities, the Supreme Court came to the following view:—
>
> > "that in a country where the population is increasing by the tick of every second on the clock and the Government had taken up the family planning as an important programme for the implementation of which it had created mass awakening for the use of various devices includes sterilization operation, the doctor as also the State must be held responsible in damages if the sterilization operation performed by him is a failure on account of his negligence, which is directly responsible for another birth in the family, creating additional economic burden on the person who had chosen to be operated upon for sterilization".

Reference may also be made to a case *Vinitha Ashok* v. *Lakshmi Hospital*[3] which was an unfortunate case of a woman losing her uterus – vital organ of regeneration – consequent upon an ectopic pregnancy in the cervical canal. The Supreme Court also relied on its earlier decision in the case of *Achutrao Haribhau Khodwa* v. *State of Maharashtra*[4] and held as under:—

> "The skill of medical practitioners differs from doctor to doctor. The very nature of the profession is such that there may be more than one course of treatment which may be advisable for treating a patient. Courts would indeed be slow in attributing negligence on the part of a doctor if he has performed his duties to the best of his ability and with due care and caution. Medical opinion may differ with regard to the course of action to be taken by a doctor treating a patient, but as long as doctor acts in a manner which is acceptable to the medical profession and the Court finds that he has attended

1. AIR 1998 SC 1801.
2. (1981) 1 All ER 267.
3. AIR 2001 SC 3915.
4. AIR 1996 SC 2377.

on the patient with due care, skill and diligence and if the patient still does not a survive or suffers a permanent ailment, it would be difficult to hold the doctor to be guilty of negligence".

Reference may be made to the latter decision of the Supreme Court in *Savita Gard* v. *Director, National Heart Institute*[1] wherein the Consumer Disputes Redressal Commission dismissed the original petition of the appellant on the ground of non-joinder of necessary party. The Supreme Court referred to the scope of the Consumer Forum in the following manner:—

> "The Consumer Forum is primarily meant to provide better protection in the interest of the consumers and not to short circuit the matter or to defeat the claim on technical grounds. Reverting back to the facts of the present case, whether non-joinder of the treating doctor and nursing staff can result a dismissal of the claim petition. As a matter of fact, when a patient is admitted to a highly commercial hospital like the present Institute, a thorough check-up of the patient is done by the hospital authorities, it is the Institute which selects, after the examination of the patient that he suffers from what malady, and who is the best doctor who can attend, except when the patient or the family members desire to be treated by a particular doctor or surgeon as the case may be. Normally, private hospitals have a panel of doctors in various specialties and it is they who choose who is to be called. It is very difficult for the patient to give any detail of which doctor treated the patient and whether the doctor was negligent or the nursing staff was negligent. It is very difficult for such patient or his relatives to implead them as parties in the claim petition. It will be an impossible task and if the claim is to be defeated on that ground it will virtually be frustrating the provisions of the Act, leaving the claimant high and dry. The patients once they are admitted to such hospitals, it is the responsibility of the said hospital or the medical institutions to satisfy that all possible care was taken and no negligence was involved in attending the patient. The burden cannot be placed on the patient to implead all those treating doctors or the attending staff of the hospital as a party so as to substantiate his claim. Once a patient is admitted in a hospital it is the responsibility of the hospital to provide the best service and if it does not, then the hospital cannot take shelter under the technical ground that the surgeon concerned or the nursing staff, as the case may be, was not impleaded, and therefore, the claim should be rejected on the basis of non-joinder of necessary parties".

1. (2004) 8 SCC 56.

The entire liabilities of Medical professionals in respect of death due to criminal medical negligence has been discussed by a Bench of three Judges in a decision of the Supreme Court in the case of *Jacob Mathew* v. *State of Punjab*.[1] In Original Petition No. 85 of 1998 the National Consumer Disputes Redressal Commission, New Delhi *vide* order dated 26-5-2010 also referred to the said judgment. The court had discussed the scope of section 2(1) (g & o) of Consumer Protection Act, 1986. The Court summoned up its conclusion in para 48 of the Jacob Mathew case in the following terms:—

(1) Negligence is the breach of duty caused by omission to do something which a reasonable man guided by those considerations which ordinarily regulate the conduct of human affairs would do, or doing something which a prudent and reasonable man would not do, or doing something which a prudent and reasonable man would not do.The definition of negligence as given in *Law of Torts, Ratanlal & Dhirajlal*, edited by Justice G.P. Singh), referred to hereinabove, holds good. Negligence becomes actionable on account of injury resulting from the act or omission amounting to negligence attributable to the person sued. The essential components of negligence are three: "duty", 'breach" and "resulting damage."

(2) Negligence in the context of the medical profession necessarily calls for a treatment with a difference. To infer rashness or negligence on the part of a professional, in particular a doctor, additional considerations apply. A case of occupational negligence is different from one of professional negligence. A simple lack of care, an error of judgment or an accident, is not proof of negligence on the part of a medical professional. So long as a doctor follows a practice acceptable to the medical profession of that day, he cannot be held liable for negligence merely because a better alternative course or method of treatment was also available or simply because a more skilled doctor would not have chosen to follow or resort to that practice or procedure which the accused followed. When it comes to the failure of taking precautions, what has to be seen is whether those precautions were taken which the ordinary experience of men has found to be sufficient; a failure to use special or extraordinary precautions which might have prevented the particular happening cannot be the standard for judging the alleged negligence. So also, the standard of care,

1. (2005) 6 SCC 1.

while assessing the practice as adopted, is judged in the light of knowledge available at the time of the incident, and not at the date of trial. Similarly, when the charge of negligence arises out of failure to use some particular equipment, the charge would fail if the equipment was not generally available at that particular time (that is, the time of the incident) at which it is suggested it should have been used.

(3) A professional may be held liable for negligence on one of the two findings: either he was not possessed of the requisite skill which he professed to have possessed, or he did not exercise, with reasonable competence in the given case, the skill which he did possess. The standard to be applied for judging, whether the person charged has been negligent or not, would be that of an ordinary competent person exercising ordinary skill in that profession. It is not possible for every professional to possess the highest level of expertise or skills in that branch which he practices. A highly skilled professional may be possessed of better qualities, but that cannot be made the basis or the yardstick for judging the performance of the professional proceeded against on indictment of negligence.

(4) The test for determining medical negligence as laid down in *Bolan* case, WLR at P.586 holds good in its applicability in India.

(5) The jurisprudential concept of negligence differs in civil and criminal law. What may be negligence in civil law may not necessarily be negligence in criminal law. For negligence to amount to an offence, the element of *mens rea* must be shown to exist. For an act to amount to criminal negligence, the degree of negligence should be much higher *i.e.*, gross or of a very high degree. Negligence which is neither gross nor of a higher degree may provide a ground for action in civil law but cannot form the basis for prosecution.

(6) The word "gross" has not been used in section 304A, IPC, yet it is settled that in criminal law negligence or recklessness, to be so held, must be of such a high degree as to be "gross". The expression 'rash or negligent act" as occurring in section 304A, IPC has to be read as qualified by word "grossly".

(7) To prosecute a medical professional for negligence under criminal law it must be shown that the accused did something or failed to do something which in the given fats and circumstances no medical professional in his ordinary senses and prudence would have done or failed to do. The hazard

taken by the accused doctor should be of such a nature that the injury which resulted was most likely imminent.

(8) *Res ipsa loquitur* is only a rule of evidence and operates in the domain of civil law, specially in cases of torts and helps in determining the onus of proof in actions relating to negligence. It cannot be pressed in service of determining *per se* the liability for negligence within the domain of criminal law. *Res ipsa loquitur* has, if at all, a limited application in trial on a charge of criminal negligence.

ELECTION LAWS AND CRIMINALISATION OF POLITICS

The present subject is of such paramount importance that the same found mention in the Presidential Address on the occasion of the Golden Jubilee celebrations of Independence of India held from 26th August to 1st September, 1997. It will be pertinent to point out to the relevant extract of the Resolution adopted by the Lok Sabha in the Special Session on the historic occasion of the Golden Jubilee of Independence.

"We the members of Lok Sabha, meeting in a specially convened Golden Jubilee Session of both Houses of Parliament to commemorate the completion of half a century of India's freedom."

"Do now solemnly affirm our joint and unanimous commitment to the issues hereinafter mentioned, and we also do solemnly resolve and direct that they be adopted as minimum tasks, constituting our 'Agenda for India' on this historic occasion."

"That meaningful electoral reforms be carried out so that the Parliament and other legislative bodies be balanced and effective instruments of democracy".

"That continuous and productive efforts be launched for ensuring greater transparency, probity and accountability in public life so that the freedom, authority and dignity of the Parliament and other legislative bodies are ensured and enhanced; that more especially, all political parties shall undertake all such steps as will attain the objective of ridding our polity of criminalisation or its influence".

Shri U.C. Aggarwal, Former Central Vigilance Commissioner in his article "Galloping Corruption: Need for Effective Vigilance" commented about recent level of corruption in the following manner: "Rampant and widespread corruption," both in the public services as also among holders of high political offices, is undoubtedly a matter of serious national concern. Although brave words to "wage war" against corruption, "no compromise" on corruption and "not to spare any corrupt person however high" have time and again, been voiced by all the top leaders of different political parties in power at the Centre and in the States but there has been little dent on corruption or corrupt individual. In fact, corruption has become more common and deep-rooted. It has also engulfed larger number of persons holding high public offices during the last one decade. It is now galloping unchecked and unhindered.

Shri M.S. Gill, the then Chief Election Commissioner of India in his article on "Role and Functioning of Election Commission of India" has pointed out that to the effective steps, being taken by the Commission in respect of preventing Criminalisation of Politics in the following manner: "Another important area into which the Commission is trying to make inroad and which is being watched by the whole nation with serious concern is the growing criminalisation of politics. The Commission has already taken its first step—a major step in this direction, on August 28, 1997, to keep the convicts out of the holy precincts of the Parliament and the State Legislatures. It was often observed that many a persons convicted of heinous crimes like murder, dacoity, rape, etc., were entering into electoral fray, and getting elected, despite being disqualified under the law (Section 8 of the Representation of People Act, 1951) for contesting elections. They became candidates under the subterfuge that they had filed appeals against their conviction, and had been released on bail during the pendency of such appeals. The Commission has now clarified to all concerned that such convicted persons are disqualified for elections, regardless of whether they are out on bail or not. All candidates, in future, will also have to furnish information about their convictions, if any, with a sworn affidavit, at the time of filing their nomination papers. The Commission is also examining further how to restructure and tighten the law, so that the lawbreakers do not become lawmakers."

In a case reported as *Anukul Chandra Pradhan* v. *Union of India,*[1] an important question answered was whether a person in imprisonment can maintain the right to vote. The Supreme Court held as under:—

> "The right to vote is a statutory right and not a common law right because of which it depends on the nature of right conferred by the statute. The right to vote is subject to the limitations imposed by the statute which can be exercised only in the manner provided by the statute; and the challenge to any provision in the statute prescribing the nature of right to elect cannot be made with reference to a fundamental right in the Constitution. The very basis of challenge to the validity of sub-section (5) of section 62 of the Act is, therefore, not available and this petition must fail"

1. AIR 1997 SC 2814.

Reference may be made to two more judgments of the Hon'ble Supreme Court. In the case reported as *Ruli Ram* v. *State of Haryana*.[1] The Supreme Court was dealing with a case, where political rivalry resulted in the death of innocent children. The Supreme Court made the following observations:

> "Political battles are increasingly being fought with bullets and not with ballots. Innocent lives are lost and in some cases of those who have no role to play therein".
>
> "The criminalization of politics is a hot topic causing concern. The election was to a panchayat in 1988. The lives of innocent children were taken. One shudders to think what happens presently, when a large number of people lose lives in the heat of political battles for election to the legislative bodies. In a democracy, the path to power cannot be allowed to have dead bodies littered over it. It cannot be a case of capturing power (beginning with booth capturing) at any cost. The trend is dangerous and has to be curbed. In a case linked with political battles, stringent punishment is desirable without exception"

Ultimately the Supreme Court held that the sentence of 10 years rigorous imprisonment awarded by the trail court is quite appropriate, the accused-appellants shall suffer rigorous imprisonment for 10 years in respect of their conviction under section 304, Part II, I.P.C.

The court in another matter relating to criminalization of politics reported as *Union of India* v. *Association for Democratic Reforms*,[2] made the following observations:—

> "During the course of hearing, we got an impression that learned counsel for all the parties, including the *Union of India* and the Election Commission of India, are agreed that there is a need to check criminalisation of politics and misuse of money or muscle power during elections. So far as this aspect is concerned, all the parties appear to be in agreement."

Constitutional Provisions

The Constitutional provisions relating to elections are provided in Part XV of the Constitution under articles 324 to 329. Article 324 of the Constitution provides for creation of Election Commission as an independent constitutional authority to supervise, direct and control the preparation of the electoral rolls and conduct of elections to the Parliament and to the Legislatures of every State, and elections to the

1. AIR 2002 SC 3360.
2. (2002) 10 SCC 111.

offices of President and Vice-President held under the Constitution. Article 325 provides for ineligibility for inclusion or to claim to be included in special electoral rolls on accounts of religion, race, caste or sex. Article 326 provides for election to the House of People and to the Legislative Assemblies of States specially on the basis of adult franchise. Articles 327 and 328 provides power of the Parliament and Legislatures of a State to make provisions with respect to election to Parliament and the State Legislatures respectively. Article 329 provides for a bar to interference by the Court in electoral matters and specifically provides that no election to either House of Parliament or either House of the Legislature of a State shall be called to question except by an election petition, as may be provided for under any law made by the appropriate authority.

It will, therefore, be seen that there is hardly any change required in the provisions relating to elections as provided in the Constitution of India.

Representation of Peoples Act, 1951

Reference may be made to the provisions of the Representation of Peoples Act regarding disqualification. Section 8 provides for disqualification on conviction for certain offences such as, offences under sections 153A, 171E, sections 376 & 376A to 376D, 498A and 505 of the Indian Penal Code. Similarly, persons convicted of offence under Foreign Exchange (Regulation) Act, 1973 or the Narcotic Drugs and Psychotropic Substances Act, 1985 or under section 3 or 4 of the Terrorist and Disruptive Activities (Prevention) Act, 1997, have been disqualified. Only the illustrative cases have been pointed out.

The said Act is silent as to what happens between the period when an appeal is pending against such conviction in the Higher Courts and/or when there is a stay of sentence or the person is on bail granted by the Higher Court including the High Court and the Supreme Court. It was this aspect which was referred to in the article by Shri M.S. Gill, then Chief Election Commissioner referred to above. The Commission had also clarified that such convicted persons are disqualified for election regardless of whether they are out on bail or not and all candidates in future will also furnish information about their conviction if any with the sworn affidavit at the time of filing their nomination papers. Similarly, section 8(2) of the said Act provides that persons convicted for contravention of law relating to prevention of hoarding, profiteering, adulteration of food or drugs, Dowry Prohibition Act, etc. shall be disqualified, only if they are sentenced to imprisonment for not less than 6 months. The restriction imposed also appears to be unrealistic as the said offences are also of serious nature and perhaps the law requires suitable amendments.

Looking at the election law, it appears that there is no prohibition or disqualification for a person who has been charge-sheeted for a serious offence like dacoity, murder, rape, etc., until and unless the person accused has been convicted of the said offence. In my opinion, persons who have been charge-sheeted for such serious offences should be debarred from contesting elections to Lok Sabha or the Legislative Assemblies. The reign of terror is let loose by the candidates who have criminal records, and it is essential that they be debarred from contesting elections.

Similarly, there should be prohibition for the candidates seeking help of known criminals or those against whom serious charges are pending and such persons should not be permitted to carry out election campaign for the candidates.

Another important aspect, which can stop criminalisation of politics is that the political parties, should themselves choose only those candidates who have no criminal record, and against whom no charge sheets, have been filed in respect of serious offences. Political Parties should invariably set standards in selecting honest and upright persons of outstanding merit to stand for elections. A great duty is cast on the political parties to rise to the occasion, so that the criminalisation of politics is banished from the Indian scene.

Unless persons of merit and outstanding ability are persuaded to stand up for elections, the future of democracy will be in danger.

Another aspect which has been agitating my mind is that the persons who have to make law for the country and the States, should be qualified people, so that they can make effective laws. Unfortunately, there are no conditions relating to educational qualifications prescribed for standing to election. The public opinion will have to be created before such changes could be considered in the law of elections. In my opinion, it would be appropriate for prescribing certain minimum levels of education before a person is elected to the Parliament or the State Assembly. It is high time that people of this country and the nation at large take an active interest in the election law so that criminalisation of politics is abolished from the national scene. A special duty is cast on those who are conversant with the law and particularly distinguished legal professionals to make valuable contributions in bringing about changes in the electoral laws so that persons of high merit and integrity are elected as members of Parliament and State Legislatures.

LIABILITY OF AUCTION PURCHASER OF PROPERTY TO PAY FOR THE OLD ELECTRICITY BILLS IN RESPECT OF THE PREMISES

An important question of law regarding the liability of an auction purchaser to meet the liability of old consumer of electricity for the premises purchased by him was raised before the Supreme Court in a recent case of *Isha Marbles* v. *Bihar State Electricity Board*.[1]

The Supreme Court negatived the contention and held that an auction purchaser who had purchased the premises in auction sale from Bihar State Financial Corporation under the Bihar State Financial Operation Act, 1951 was not liable for the same. The facts in the main case were that Isha Marbles purchased the mortgaged assets of Patel Industries, Daltonganj in an open auction held under the Corporation Act and paid a substantial sum towards the said transaction and got possession of the said unit and was called upon to discharge all the liabilities of the previous consumer. This was challenged before the High Court of Patna, Ranchi Bench and it was urged that there was a transfer of a Unit, it had not even been supplied with electricity and hence was no occasion to consume electricity and the transferee is not liable for energy consumed before such transfer. The writ petition was dismissed by the Division Bench of the High Court against which appeal was filed before the Supreme Court.

In a connected case, however, it was held that the Board (Bihar State Electricity Board) was under a statutory obligation to supply electricity energy to any person whenever a requisition is made subject to the fulfilment of certain conditions under clause 6 of the Schedule 1 of the Electricity Act, it was held by the Court that the Board is a "State" within the meaning of article 12 of the Constitution and therefore disconnection must pass the test of fairness and reasonableness, and in that case the petition was allowed, and a writ of *mandamus* was issued to the Board, to provide electricity connection on the terms and conditions laid down in

1. JT 1995 (2) SC 626: (1995) 2 SCC 648.

the Electricity Act. In that case it was held that the petitioner was a *bona fide* purchaser under statutory sale. It was also held that the agreement entered into between the consumer and the buyer contained personal bond as between the parties to the agreement and the Board cannot take advantage of its own wrong in allowing the arrears to get accumulated.

Various contentions were raised by the Appellant in the main appeal including the one that he was a *bona fide* purchaser of the assets of the mortgaged industries in an auction sale and he was neither the transferee nor the successor to the previous owner of the premises and was an independent buyer, he was not a consumer and he cannot be held to be a consumer since factually the Appellant was yet to be given electricity connection.

It was also argued that section 24 of the Indian Electricity Act, 1910 was not applicable and the Appellant could not be held liable for any default committed by the previous consumer. Various decisions of the High Court were cited in support of these contentions.

In support of this submission reliance was placed on *Sauriyar Luka* v. *Kerala Electricity Board.*[1] In that case, the test applied was whether the applicant seeking electricity connection is a legal representative of the defaulter. Further, the payment of arrears due from the defaulting consumer could be insisted upon for the supply of electricity to the premises used by the erstwhile consumer.

The Supreme Court held that the relationship between the Board and a consumer is purely contractual, relying on the decision in *Bihar State Electricity Board* v. *Green Rubber Industries.*[2]

The Supreme Court held that the following were the indisputable facts:

1. The previous units had the benefits of electricity supply.
2. The previous units/owners had borrowed from the corporation.
3. To secure those loans they had mortgaged/hypothecated the properties.
4. The electricity arrears in relation to these premises had fallen due since they had neglected to pay.
5. By exercise of power under section 24 of the Electricity Act the electricity was disconnected.

---

1. AIR 1959 Ker 199.
2. (1990) 1 SCC 731.

6. For recovery of the loans the mortgaged/hypothecated properties were brought to sale under section 28 of the Corporation Act.

The Supreme Court referred to the important provisions of the Indian Electricity Act, 1910 and the Electricity (Supply) Act, 1948, and held that the law relating to electricity is principally contained in these two Acts. The Supreme Court referred to the various provisions of the aforesaid Acts. Regarding the requirements for getting electricity supply, for premises, the Supreme Court referred to Shiv Gopal's law, relating to Electricity and held that the auction purchaser came to purchase the property after disconnection and cannot be a consumer or occupier within the meaning of the provision of law. The Supreme Court also held as under:

> "Electricity is public property. Law, in its majesty, highly protects public property and behoves every one to respect public property. But, the law, as it stands is inadequate to enforce the liability of the previous contracting party against the auction purchaser who is a third party and is in no way connected with the previous owners/occupier."

The Supreme Court affirmed the decision in *Sauriyar Luka* v. *Kerala Electricity Board,*[1] on which reliance was placed by the counsel for *Isha Marbles.*[2]

However, the Court cautioned that dishonest consumers cannot be allowed to play truant with the public property but inadequacy of the law can hardly be substituted by over-zealousness.

The Supreme Court case *Isha Marbles* v. *Bihar State Electricity Board,*[2] came up for review before the Hon'ble Supreme Court in a later case reported as *Ahmedabad Electricity Co. Ltd.* v. *Gujrat Inns Pvt. Ltd.*[3] The Supreme Court reaffirmed its earlier decision in the following manner:—

> "We are clearly of the opinion that in case of a fresh connection though the premises are the same, the auction-purchasers cannot be held liable to clear the arrears incurred by the previous owners in respect of power supply to the premises in the absence of there being a specific statutory provision in that regard".

The court declined to reconsider the wide proposition of law laid down in *Isha Marbles'* case in the following manner:—

1. AIR 1959 Ker 199.
2. (1995) 2 SCC 648.
3. AIR 2004 SC 2171.

> "Though we find some merit in the submission of the learned Counsel for the appellant calling for reconsideration of the wide propositions of law laid down in *Isha Marbles'* case. We think the present one is not a case for such exercise. We leave the plea open for consideration in an appropriate case".

The judgments mentioned above are landmark judgments not only with respect to consumers of electricity in the State of Bihar, Ahmedabad but also for general consumers in the rest of the country. It has become a normal feature that wrong bills are sent to the purchasers of property and/or to persons in occupation of the same, in respect of electricity consumed for which they could not be held responsible in any way. The supply of electricity being essential commodity in the present times, it is all the more important that consumers not be penalized for electricity not consumed by them and for which they are in no way responsible, and it is high time that the electricity departments wake up to this reality.

OBSCENITY AND THE LAW: THE CASE OF THE "BANDIT QUEEN"

An important and landmark judgment of the Supreme Court, relating to the release of the film "Bandit Queen", *Bobby Art International* v. *Om Pal Singh Hoon*[1] decided on 1-5-1996. The release of the film "Bandit Queen" has created interest and was the subject-matter of litigation in the Delhi High Court and ultimately the matter was disposed of by the Hon'ble Supreme Court of India by a Bench consisting of A.M. Ahmadi, C.J.I., S.P. Bharucha and B.N. Kirpal, JJ. The facts of the case as also summarized in judgment of the Supreme Court were as under:—

'Bandit Queen' is the story of a village child exposed from an early age to the brutality and lust of man. Married off to a man old enough to be her father she is beaten and raped. The village boys make advances which she repulses; but the village panchayat finds her guilty of the enticement of a village boy because he is of high caste and she has to leave the village. She is arrested and, in the police station, filthily abused. Those who stand bail for her do so to satisfy their lust. She is kidnapped and raped. During an act of brutality the rapist is shot dead and she finds an ally in her rescuer. With his assistance she beats up her husband, violently. Her rescuer is shot dead by one whose advances she has spurned. She is gang-raped by the rescuer's assailant and his accomplices and they humiliate her in the sight of the village; a hundred men stand in a circle around the village well and watch the humiliation, her being stripped naked and walked around the circle and then made to draw water. And not one of the villagers help her. She burns with anger, shame and the urge for vengeance. She gets it, and kills many Thakurs too.

The film was based on a book written by Mala Sen called "India's Bandit Queen" and has been in the market since the year 1991 without objection.

On 17th August, 1994 the film was presented for certification to the Censor Board under the Cinematographs Act, 1952. The Examining Committee of the Censor Board referred it to the Revising Committee

1. JT 1996 (4) SC 533.

under rule 24(1) of the Cinemagographic (Certification) Rules, 1983. On 19th July, 1995, the Revising Committee recommended that the film be granted an 'A' certificate, subject to certain excisions and modifications. (An 'A' certificate implies that the film may be viewed only by adults).

An appeal was filed under section 5C of the Cinematographs Act before the Appellate Tribunal constituted under section 5 of the Cinematographs Act which consists of a Chairman and members who are required to judge the effect of the film on the public. The Tribunal was Chaired by Justice Lenton, retired Judge of the Bombay High Court and three ladies Smt. Sara Mohammad, Dr. Sarayu V. Doshi and Smt. Reena Kumar. Upon the basis of the unanimous orders of the Tribunal the film was granted an 'A' certificate. The film was screened on 31st August, 1995 at Siri Fort Auditorium on the occasion of the 27th International Film Festival of India and open to public viewing at various cinema theatres in the country. However, on 27th January, 1996, a writ petition was filed before the Delhi High Court seeking to quash the certificate granted to the film. The learned Single Judge allowed the writ petition and quashed the certificate granted to it and directed the Censor Board to consider the grant of 'A' certificate to it after excision and modifications in accordance with the order and the screening of the film was injuncted till the fresh certificate was granted. An appeal was filed before the Division Bench of the Delhi High Court and view of the learned Single Judge was upheld. Against the judgment of the Division Bench appeal was filed in the Supreme Court.

The Supreme Court referred to the provisions of section 5 of the Cinematographs Act, which virtually echoes articles 19(2) of the Constitution. The Supreme Court also referred to the guidelines earlier issued under the Cinematographs Act in the year 1990-91. The Supreme Court referred to its earlier decisions.

K.B. Abbas v. *Union of India*,[1] wherein the controversy related to a documentary film entitled "Tale of 4 Cities". The Supreme, Court held that it is not the element of rape, leprosy, sexual immorality which attract the Censor and scissors but how the theme is handled by the producer. The Supreme Court also referred to its earlier judgment in *Raj Kapoor* v. *State*,[2] wherein the Supreme Court was dealing with a *pro bono publico* petition against the producer, actors and other connected with a film called *Satyam Shivam Sundaram*. The Supreme Court referred to the following passage:

> "Art, morals and law's manacles on aesthetics are a sensitive subject where jurisprudence meets other social sciences and never

1. (1970) 2 SCC 780.
2. (1980) 1 SCC 43.

goes alone to bark and bite because State-made straight jacket is an inhibitive prescription for a free country unless enlightened society actively participates in the administration of justice to aesthetics."

Similarly, the Supreme Court referred to the case of *Samaresh Bose* v. *Amal Mitra*,[1] wherein the Court was concerned with a novel entitled *Prajapati*.

The Court also referred to the case of *State of Bihar* v. *Shailbala Devi*,[2] wherein Justice Mahajan said:

> "That a writing had to be considered as a whole and in a fair and free and liberal spirit, and an endeavour had to be made to gather the general effect which the whole composition would have on the mind of the public."

In *Sakal Paper (P) Ltd.* v. *Union of India*,[3] a Constitution Bench held that the only restrictions which can be imposed on the rights of an individual under article 19(1)(a) were those which clause (2) of article 19 permitted and no other. This was reiterated in *Life Insurance Corporation of India* v. *Prof. Manubhai D. Shah*.[4]

The Supreme Court summarized that the guidelines required the authorities concerned that film certification be responsive to the values and standards of the society and take note of social change and they are required to ensure that artistic expression and creative freedom are not unduly curbed. The film must be judged in its entirety from the point of view of its overall impact. It must also be judged in the light of the period depicted and the contemporary standards of the people to whom it relates but it must not deprave the morality of the audience.

The Supreme Court applying the said test held that the Tribunal had viewed the film in true perspective and had in compliance with the requirement of the guidelines granted to the film an 'A' certificate subject to the conditions it stated. The appeals were accordingly allowed and the judgment and order made by the High Court set aside and the writ petitions were dismissed. The 'A' certificate, issued to the film *Bandit Queen* upon the conditions imposed by the Appellate Tribunal, was restored.

Reference may be made to a later decision of the Supreme Court in *Directorate General of Doordarshan* v. *Anand Patwardhan*.[5] The facts of the case as narrated in the judgment are as under:—

---

1. (1985) 4 SCC 289.
2. 1952 SCR 654.
3. (1962) 3 SCR 842.
4. JT 1992 (4) SC 181: (1992) 3 SCC 637.
5. (2006) 8 SCC 433.

"The appellant in the present matter is Doordarshan who have decided not to telecast the documentary film made by the respondent titled 'Father, Son and Holy War'. The respondent is a filmmaker. Respondent 1 in 1995 submitted his documentary film, "Father, Son and Holy War", to the appellant for telecast on national network Doordarshan. Respondent 1 was to provide a U-matic certificate for the same to be aired by Doordarshan".

"On 11-7-2003, the Prasar Bharati Board previewed the documentary film and was of the opinion that the documentary film contained scenes which could promote violence, its production quality was unsatisfactory and its telecast would be violative of the policy of Doordarshan of not screening 'A' certified movies. This decision of Doordarshan was communicated to Respondent 1 on 18-7-2003".

"The respondent filed a writ petition in the Bombay High Court which directed Doordarshan to exhibit the documentary film of Respondent 1, "Father, Son and Holy War on Channel I or II within 12 weeks from the date of the judgment on a convenient day and time as fixed by Doordarshan. It is against this decision of the High Court of Bombay, Doordarshan has come in appeal to this Court."

The judgment referred to the definition of obscenity in the Encyclopedia stated as under—

> "By English law it is an indictable misdemeanour to show an obscene exhibition or to publish any obscene matter, whether it be in writing or by pictures, effigy or otherwise. The precise meaning of 'obscene' is, however, decidedly ambiguous. It has been defined as something offensive to modesty or decency, or expressing or suggesting unchaste or lustful ideas or being impure, indecent or lewd".

The Supreme Court also referred to case law in the United States and held as under:—

> "Therefore, one can observe that the basic guidelines for the tier of fact must be:
>
> (a) whether "the average person, applying contemporary community standards" would find that the work taken as a whole, appeals to the prurient interest.......
>
> (b) whether the work depicts or describes, in a patently offensive way, sexual conduct specifically defined by the applicable State Law, and
>
> (c) whether the work, taken as a whole, lacks serious literary, artistic, political, or scientific value".

Ultimately the Supreme Court came to the following conclusion:—

"In our opinion, the respondent has a right to convey his perception on the oppression of women, flawed understanding of manhood and evils of communal violence through the documentary film produced by him. As already noticed, this film has won awards for best investigative film and best film on social issues at the national level as well. The freedom of expression, which is legitimate and constitutionally protected, cannot be held to ransom on a mere fall of a hat. The film in its entirety has a serious message to convey and is relevant in the present context. Doordarshan being a State controlled agency funded by public funds could not have denied access to screen the respondent's documentary except on specified valid grounds".

Lastly a reference has been made to a decision reported as *Ajay Goswamy* v. *Union of India*.[1] The Supreme Court in a monumental judgment referred to Press Council's Act, 1978 section 13(2)(c), 14(1) and 14(2). The Court also referred to section 292 of the Penal Code and sections 4 and 5 of the Indecent Representation of Women (Prohibition) Act, 1886. The judgment also referred to earlier decisions of the Supreme Court in the case reported as *Director General of Doordarshan* v. *Anand Patwardhan*[2] and also to a decision in *Chanderkant Kalyandas Kakodhar* v. *State of Maharashtra*[3] and a decision in a case *Samresh Bose* v. *Amal Mitra*.[4]

The Supreme Court also held that *per se* nudity is not obscenity and referred to a decision of the American Courts in this connection. The Supreme Court therefore, held that the pictures in dispute had been published by the respondent with the intent to inform readers of the current entertainment news from around the world and India. This judgment is also a land mark judgment in relation to the freedom to press and law relating to obscenity.

Reference may also be made to the most recent judgment decided on 4-2-2010 by the Bench of Hon'ble Mr. Justice Deepak Verma & Hon'ble Dr. Justice B.S. Chauhan, titled as *S. Khushboo* v. *Kanniammal* in Crl. A. 913/2010.

The facts of the case are as under:—

The Appellant is a well known actress who has approached this court to seek quashing of criminal proceedings pending against her. As many as 23 criminal complaints were filed against her, mostly in the State of Tamil Nadu, for the offences contemplated under

1. (2007) 1 SCC 143.
2. (2006) 8 SCC 433.
3. (1969) 2 SCC 687.
4. (1985) 4 SCC 289.

sections 499, 500 and 505 of the Indian Penal Code, 1860 (hereinafter 'IPC') and sections 4 and 6 of the Indecent Representation of Women (Prohibition) Act, 1986. The trigger for the same were some remarks made by the appellant in an interview to a leading news magazine and later on the same issue was reported in a distorted manner in another periodical. Faced with the predicament of contesting the criminal proceedings instituted against her in several locations, the appellant had approached the High Court of Madras, praying for the quashing of these proceedings through the exercise of its inherent power under section 482 of the Code of Criminal Procedure, 1973. The High Court rejected her plea *vide* impugned judgment and order dated 30-4-2008.

The statement which was published and the basis of the action taken against her have also been reproducing in the judgment as under:—

"According to me, sex is not only concerned with the body; but also concerned with the conscious. I could not understand matters such as changing boy friends every week. When a girl is committed to her boyfriend, she can tell her parents and go out with him. When their daughter is having a serious relationship, the parents should allow the same. Our society should come out of the thinking that at the time of the marriage, the girls should be with virginity. None of the educated men, will expect that the girl whom they are marrying should be with virginity. But when having sexual relationship the girls should protect themselves from conceiving and getting venereal diseases."

There was also conversation between the appellant and a correspondent from'Dhina Thanthi' which are as under:—

"The persons who are protesting against my interview, are talking about which culture? Is there anyone who does not know about the sex in Tamil Nadu? Is there anyone who does not know about AIDS? How many men and women do not have sex before marriage? Why are people saying after the marriage the husband and wife should be honest and faithful to each other? One should have confidence in the other, only to avoid the mistakes from being committed. If the husband, without the knowledge of the wife, or the wife, without the knowledge of the husband, have sex with other persons, if a disease is caused through that, the same will affect both the persons. It will also affect the children. Only because of this, they are saying like that. "However, soon after the publication of the above mentioned news item, the appellant had sent a legal notice dated 2-10-2005 to the Editor of "Dhina Thanti'. Categorically denying that she had made the statement quoted above.

The entire case law relating to obscenity was discussed by the Hon'ble Supreme Court particularly the following Judgments were referred:—

Ranjit D. Udeshi v. *State of Maharashtra;*[1]

Samaresh Bose v. *Amal Mitra;*[2]

Lata Singh v. *State of Uttar Pradesh;*[3]

> Wherein it was observed that a live-in relationship between two consenting adults of heterogenic sex does not amount to any offence (with the obvious exception of 'adultery'), even though it may be perceived as immoral. A major girl is free to marry anyone she likes or "live with anyone she likes", ...

This court had entertained a writ petition and granted relief by quashing the criminal trial. Furthermore, the court had noted that 'no offence was committed by any of the accused and whole criminal case in question is an abuse of the process of the court. It would also be instructive to refer to a decision of the House of Lords (U.K.) in *Gillick* v. *West Norfolk and Wisbech Area health Authority*[4] This decision supports the reasoning that we must fully understand the context and the purpose for which references to sex have been made in any given setting.

The court ultimately expresses its view that the institution of the numerous criminal complaints against the appellant was done in a *mala fide* manner. In order to prevent the abuse of criminal law machinery, we are therefore inclined to grant the relief sought by the appellant. In such cases, the proper course for Magistrates is to use their statutory powers to direct an investigation into the allegations before taking cognizance of the offences alleged. It is not the task of the Criminal Law to punish individuals merely for expressing unpopular views.

In conclusion, the Hon'ble Supreme Court find that the various complaints filed against the Appellant do not support or even draw a *prima facie* case for any of the statutory offences as alleged. Therefore, the appeals are allowed and the impugned judgment and order of the High Court dated 30-4-2008 is set aside. The impugned Criminal Proceedings are hereby quashed.

---

1. AIR 1965 SC 881.
2. AIR 1986 SC 967.
3. AIR 2006 SC 2522.
4. (1985) 3 All ER 402.

THE LAW OF ARRESTS

The question of arrest by the police which has become a source of oppression and abuse, came up for decision before the Supreme Court recently in a case reported as JT 1994 (3) SC 423. The Supreme Court referred to the expanding role of the Human Rights and also took notice of the crimes increasing rate. The Supreme Court held as under:—

> "A realistic approach should be made in this direction. The law of arrest is one of balancing individual rights, liberties and privileges, on the one hand, and individual duties, obligations and responsibilities on the other, of weighing and balancing the rights, liberties and privileges of the single individual and those of individuals collectively ......"

The Supreme Court made reference to the following observations of Mr. Justice Cardozo in the case of *People* v. *Deore*[1]:

> ".....the question is whether protection for the individual would not be gained at a disproportionate loss of protection for society. On the one side is the social need that crime shall be repressed. On the other, the social need that law shall not be flouted by the insolence of office. There are dangers in any choice. The rule of the *Adams* case *People* v. *Adams*,[2] strikes a balance between opposing interests. We must hold it to be the law until those organs of government by which a change of public policy is normally effected shall give notice to the courts that change has come to pass."

The Supreme Court also made reference to observations of learned Judge Hand *Fraed (in re:)*. The Supreme Court held that the quality of a Nation's civilisation can be largely measured by the method it uses for enforcement of Criminal law. Reference was also made to the decision of the Supreme Court in the case of *Nandini Satpati* v. *P.L. Dani*.[3] The Court also made reference to the National Pay Commission's third report.

---

1. 242 NY 13: 150 NE 585.
2. 176 NY 351: 68 NE 636 (1903).
3. AIR 1978 SC 1025.

The Supreme Court also made reference to section 58 of the Code of Criminal Procedure with respect to the apprehension of juvenile offenders, and also section 19(a) of the Children's Act. After noticing the police powers of arrest, detention and interrogation in England the Court also referred to the report of the National Police Commission in matters of making arrest. Ultimately, the Supreme Court held that for effective enforcement of the Fundamental Rights guaranteed under articles 21 and 22(1) of the Constitution of India the following requirements are to be met by the police authorities.

1. An arrested person being held in custody is entitled, if he so requests, to have one friend, relative or other person who is known to him or likely to take an interest in his welfare told as far as is practicable that he has been arrested and where he is being detained.

2. The Police Officer shall inform this right to the arrested person when he is brought to the police station.

3. An entry shall be required to be made in the Diary as to who was informed of the arrest. These protections from power must be held to follow from articles 21 and 22(1) and enforced strictly.

The Supreme Court further held that:

> "It shall be the duty of the Magistrate, before whom the arrested person is produced, to satisfy himself that these requirements have been complied with."

It was further directed that:

> "the above requirements shall be followed in all cases of arrest till legal provisions are made in this behalf, these requirements shall be in addition to the rights of the arrested persons found in the various Police Manuals."
>
> The Supreme Court concluded by pointing out that these requirements are not exhaustive and further directed that the Director-General of Police of all the States in India shall issue necessary instructions requiring due observations of these requirements. Further it was directed that departmental instructions shall also be issued that police officer making arrest should also record in the case diary the reasons for making the arrest.

The question of guidelines in connection with the arrest by police again came up for consideration before the Supreme Court in the case of *Ahmed Noormohmed Bhatii* v. *State of Gujarat.*[1] The Supreme Court referred to the earlier decisions in *Joginder Kumar* v. *State of Uttar Pradesh.*[2] The Supreme Court referred to the following observations made in the case:—

1. AIR 2005 SC 2115.
2. (1994) 4 SCC 462.

"The horizon of human rights is expanding. At the same time, the crime ràte is also increasing. Of late, this Court has been receiving complaints about violation of human rights because of indiscriminate arrests. How are we to strike a balance between the two? A realistic approach should be made in this direction. The law of arrest is one of balancing individual rights, liberties and privileges, on the one hand, and individual duties, obligations and responsibilities on the other, of weighing and balancing the rights, liberties and privileges of the single individual and those of individuals collectively: of simply deciding what is wanted and where to put the weight and the emphasis: of deciding which comes first- the criminal or society, the law violator or the law abider; of meeting the challenge which Mr. Justice Cardozo so forthrightly met when he wrestled with a similar task of balancing individual rights against society's rights and wisely held that the exclusion rule was bad law, that society came first, and that the criminal should not go free because the constable blundered....."

The Supreme Court also noticed the requirements for effective enforcement of the Fundamental Rights, inherent in article 21 and 22(1) of the Constitution of India in the following manner:—

" (1) An arrested person being held in custody is entitled, if he so requests to have one friend, relative or other person who is known to him or likely to take an interest in his welfare told as far as is practicable that he has been arrested arid where he is being detained.

(2) The police officer shall inform the arrested person when he is brought to the police station of this right.

(3) An entry shall be required to be made in the diary as to who was informed of the arrest. These protection from power must be held to flow from articles 21 and 22(1) and enforced strictly"

The Supreme Court also referred to the guidelines laid down in the case of *D.K. Basu* v. *State of West Bengal*[1] and further held as under:—

"These requirements are in addition to the constitutional and statutory safeguards and do not detract from various directions given by the Courts from time to time in connection with the safeguarding of the rights and dignity of the arrestee. This Court has also cautioned that failure to comply with the requirements aforesaid, shall apart from rendering the official concerned liable for departmental action, also render him liable to be punished for Contempt of Court".

1. (1997) 1 SCC 416.

In this view of the matter, the Supreme Court held that there was no substance in the contention that section 151 of the Code of Criminal Procedure is unconstitutional and *ultra-vires.*

The judgment of the Supreme Court are landmark judgments about the rights of the citizens in matters relating to arrest by the police and provides for the various safeguards to avoid oppression and abuse by the police of this draconian power of making arrests.

REVIEW OF THE WORD 'INDUSTRY' BY THE LARGER BENCH*

A Bench of the Supreme Court has called for re-examination of the questions decided by the Supreme Court in the famous *Bangalore Water Supply* case relating to the interpretation of word "industry" used in section 2(j) of the Industrial Disputes Act. The constitutional Bench of 7 Judges had given wide and sweeping interpretation to the word "industry" and the Industrial Disputes Act was held to cover professional clubs, educational institutions, co-operatives, research institutions, charitable projects and anything which could be looked upon as organised activity where there was relationship of employer and employees and goods were produced or service was rendered, even the local bodies could be considered as an industry.

The learned Judges comprising the Bench in the recent case of *Coir Board, E. Cochin* v. *IDPS*,[1] referred a case where an organization is run by voluntary social workers for generous and different motives particularly for the weaker sections of the society like destitute women, etc. The learned Judges also referred to other activities undertaken in the spirit of community service such as charitable hospitals. The Bench considered the earlier cases decided by the Supreme Court, wherein the word "industry" as defined in section 2(j) of the Industrial Disputes Act, 1947 had been interpreted. The Court also examined earlier cases of *Corporation of City of Nagpur* v. *Its Employees*[2]; *State of Bombay* v. *Hospital Mazdoor Sabha*[3]; *Workmen of Indian Standards Institute* v. *Management of Indian Standards Institute*[4], wherein wide connotation was given to the word "industry", since the Industrial Disputes Act was a welfare legislation for welfare of

---

* *Bangalore Water* case has been referred to a larger Bench by the decision of the Supreme Court in the case of the *State of Uttar Pradesh* v. *Jaibir Singh*, decided on May 5, 2005 and reported in the (2005) 5 SCC 1, by a Bench of 5 Judges.

1. JT 1998 (2) SC 332.
2. (1960) 2 SCR 942.
3. AIR 1960 SC 610.
4. AIR 1976 SC 145.

the workers. In the case of the workmen of *Indian Standards Institute*, it was held that the Indian Standards Institute was an Industry. There have been another set of cases of the Supreme Court and the High Court where a slightly more restricted and conventional meaning has been given to the term "Industry" as defined in the Industrial Disputes Act. In the case of *National Union Commercial Employees* v. *Meher Industrial Tribunal, Bombay*,[1] it was held that a liberal profession such as that of an attorney was not an industry because the attorney does not carry out his profession with the active co-operation of his employees and brings to bear his intellectual equipment on the work he does. The Bench also referred to the case of *University of Delhi* v. *Ram Nath*,[2] wherein the Supreme Court had held that Educational Institution is not an industry. Similarly, in the case of *Secretary, Madras Gymkhana Club Employees' Union* v. *Management of the Gymkhana Club*,[3] the Court held that club was not an industry, since its services were to the members themselves for their own pleasure and amusement and material goods were for their own consumption, and it was self serving organisation and was not an industry. The Bench also cited the judgment in the case of *Cricket Club of India* v. *Bombay Labour Union*,[4] wherein it was held that the Cricket Club of India was not an industry. In the case of *Management of Safdarjung Hospital, New Delhi* v. *Kuldip Singh Sethi*,[5] a Bench of 6 Judges of the Supreme Court unanimously followed the ratio of the *Madras Gymkhana Club's* case and held that the Safdarjung Hospital was not an industry. However, the views which were reaffirmed in *Safdarjung Hospital* by a decision of 6 Judges of the Supreme Court as well as *University of Delhi's* case were overruled in 1978 by a decision of the Bench of 7 Judges of the Supreme Court in the case of *Bangalore Water Supply and Sewerage Board* v. *A. Rajappa*[6] by a majority of five with two dissenting. The majority laid down the 'dominant nature' test for deciding whether the establishment is an industry or not. In the recent case of *Physical Research Laboratory* v. *K.G. Sharma*,[7] the Supreme Court came to the conclusion that Physical Research Laboratory was not an industry. The Bench after analyzing the various judgments held as under:—

> "Looking to the uncertainty prevailing in this area and in the light of the experience of the last two decades in applying the test laid

---

1. AIR 1962 SC 1980.
2. (1963) 2 LLJ 335.
3. AIR 1968 SC 554.
4. AIR 1969 SC 276.
5. AIR 1970 SC 1407.
6. (1978) 2 SCC 213.
7. JT 1997 (4) SC 527: (1997) 4 SCC 257.

down in the case of *Bangalore Water Supply and Sewerage Board,* re-examined it. The experience of the last two decades does not appear to be entirely happy. Instead of leading industrial peace and welfare of the community (which was the avowed purpose of artificially extending the definition of industry), the application of the Industrial Disputes Act to organisations which were quite possibly not intended to be so covered by the machinery set up under the Industrial Disputes Act, might have done more damage than good, not merely to the organisations but also to employees by the curtailment of employment opportunities."

The Hon'ble Judges directed that the matter be placed before the Hon'ble Chief Justice of India to consider whether the larger Bench should be constituted to reconsider the decision of this Court in *Bangalore Water Supply and Sewerage Board.*

Again the matter came up before a Bench comprising of 5 Judges in the case *State of Uttar Pradesh* v. *Jaibir Singh,*[1] the Supreme Court reviewed all the earlier decisions on the subject. The Supreme Court also referred to the scope of "sovereign functions" and held as under:—

"The concept of sovereignty in a constitutional democracy is different from the traditional concept of sovereignty which is confined to "law and order", "defence", "law making" and "justice dispensation". In a democracy governed by the Constitution the sovereignty vests in the people and the State is obliged to discharge its constitutional obligations contained in the directive principles of State Policy in Part IV of the Constitution of India. From that point of view, wherever the Government undertakes public welfare activities in discharge of its constitutional obligations, as provided in Part IV of the Constitution, such activities should be treated as activities in discharge of sovereign functions falling outside the purview of "industry".

The Supreme Court further held as under:—

"In response to *Bangalore Water Supply & Sewerage Board* case Parliament intervened and substituted the definition of "industry" by including within its meaning some activities of the Government and excluding some other specified governmental activities and "public utility services" involving sovereign functions. For the past 23 years, the amended definition has remained unenforced on the statute-book. The Government has been experiencing difficulty in bringing into effect the new definition. Issuance of notification as required by sub-section (2) of section 1 of the (Amendment) Act,

1. (2005) 5 SCC 1.

1982 has been withheld so far. It is, therefore, high time for the court to re-examine the judicial interpretation given by it to the definition of "industry".

The Supreme Court also referred to the decisions in a case of *Safdarjung Hospital* v. *Kuldip Singh Sethi.*[1] It was a decision of the 6 judges who agreed with the following observations:—

> "But in the collocation of the terms and their definitions these terms have a definite economic content of a particular type and on the authorities of this Court have been uniformly accepted as excluding professions and are only concerned with the production, distribution and consumption of wealth and the production and availability of material services. Industry has thus been accepted to mean only trade and business, manufacturing, or undertaking analogous to trade or business for the production of material goods or wealth and material services."

The six Judges Bench unanimously upheld the observations in *Secy., Madras Gymkhana Club Employees' Union* v. *Gymkhana Club.*[2]

> "Before the work engaged in can be described as an industry, it must bear the definite character of 'trade' or 'business' or manufacture' or 'calling' or must be capable of being described as an undertaking resulting in material goods or material services."

In this view of the matter it was again directed that the cases be now placed before Hon'ble Chief Justice of India for constituting a suitable larger Bench for reconsideration of the judgment of this Court in the case of *Bangalore Water.*

Whether the organisation run by voluntary social workers would come within the scope of Industrial Disputes Act, and also similar activities of private hospitals and associations engaged in charitable work etc., would be covered by the provision of Industrial Disputes Act, is the moot question raised. This question will be re-opened for consideration by a larger Bench of the Supreme Court. This latest judgment of the Bench of the Supreme Court which seeks to reopen the decision of the Bench of 7 Judges in the case of *Bangalore Water Supply and Sewerage Board* v. *A. Rajappa,*[3] which has held the field for the last 20 years, is a landmark judgment, as it raises questions of fundamental importance, in the field of Industrial Law.

---

1. (1970) 1 SCC 735.
2. AIR 1968 SC 554.
3. (1978) 2 SCC 213.

LAW OF TORTS

Liability of the State for the acts of its employees

The question of liability of the Government for the acts of its employees which result in injury and damage to any person came up for consideration in *Jay Luxmi Salt Works (P) Ltd.* v. *State of Gujarat*.[1] The Supreme Court examined in great detail the meaning and scope of the law of torts and gave it a very expanded meaning.

The dictionary meaning of 'Torts' is 'breach of duty leading to damage.' Same meaning attaches to it in law. Salmond has defined it as:

> "a civil wrong for which the remedy is a common law action for unliquidated damages and which is not exclusively the breach of a contract or the breach of a trust or other merely equitable obligation."

Winfield has defined tortuous liability as a liability arising from breach of a duty primarily fixed by law, this duty is towards persons generally and its breach is redressable by an action for unliquidated damages. In general, torts consist of some act done without just cause or excuse. The Law of Torts exists for the purpose of preventing men from hurting one another whether in respect of their property, their person, their reputation or anything which is theirs. Injury and damage are two basic ingredients of tort. Although these may be found in contract as well but the violations which may result into tortuous liability are breach of duty primarily fixed by the law while in contract they are fixed by the parties themselves. Further in tort the duty is towards persons generally. In contract it is towards specific person or persons. An action for tort is usually a claim for pecuniary compensation in respect of damages suffered as a result of the invasion of a legally protected interest.

The Supreme Court observed that the liability of torts being a developing law its frontiers are incapable of being strictly barricaded. Liability in tort which in course of time has come to be known as 'strict

1. JT 1994 (3) SC 492.

liability,' 'absolute liability' or 'special use bringing with it increased dangers to other' *Rylands* v. *Fletcher*,[1] and 'fault liability' are different forms which give rise to action in torts. The distance between 'strict liability' and 'fault liability' arises from presence and absence of mental element.

A breach of legal duty wilfully or deliberately or even maliciously is negligence emanating from fault liability but injury or damage resulting without any intention yet due to lack of foresight etc., is strict liability. Since duty is the primary yardstick to determine the tortuous liability its ambit keeps on widening on the touchstone of fairness, practicality of the situation etc. In *Donoghue* v. *Stevenson*,[2] a manufacturer was held to be liable to ultimate consumer on the principle of duty to care. In *Anns* v. *Merton London Borough Council*,[3] it was rightly observed:

> "The broad general principle of liability for foreseeable damage is so widely applicable that the function of the duty of care is not so much to identify cases where liability is imposed as to identify those where it is not."

The Supreme Court even gave it an extended meaning and found that the law of torts was founded and structured on morality that no one has a right to injure or harm other intentionally or even innocently. The Supreme Court further held, therefore, that it would be primitive to close strictly or close finally the ever-expanding and growing horizon of tortuous liability. Even for social development, orderly growth of the society and cultural refineness, the liberal approach to tortuous liability by courts is more conducive.

---

1. 1968 LR (3) 330.
2. (1932) AC 562.
3. (1978) AC 728.

CORRUPTION IN HIGH PLACES—VIEWS OF SUPREME COURT

"Corruption is one of the most talked about subjects today in the country since it is believed to have penetrated into every sphere of activity. It is described as wholly widespread and spectacular."

Corruption as such has reached dangerous heights and dangerous potentialities. The word 'corruption' has wide connotation and embraces almost all the spheres of our day-to-day life the world over. In a limited sense it connotes allowing decisions and actions of a person to be influenced not by rights or wrongs of a cause, but by the prospects of monetary gains or other selfish considerations. Avarice is a common frailty of mankind, and while Robert Walpole's observation that every man has a price, may be a little generalised, yet it cannot be gainsaid is not far from truth. Burke cautioned "Among a people generally corrupt, liberty cannot last long". *State of Andhra Pradesh* v. *Vasudeva Rao.*[1]

Reference may be made to the famous JMM bribery case involving the then Prime Minister *P.V. Narasimha Rao* v. *State,*[2] regarding the question whether Member of Parliament is a public servant for the purpose of Prevention of Corruption Act, 1988. The Court held as under:—

> "Having considered the submission of the learned counsel on the meaning of the expression 'public servant' as contained in section 2(c) of the 1988 Act, we are of the view that a Member of Parliament is a public servant for the purpose of the 1988 Act".

Reference may be made to *TANSI Corrupton* case, *R. Sai Bharti* v. *J. Jayalalitha, Chief Minister of Tamil Nadu.*[3] The facts of the case were: "a private complaint was lodged before the IX Metropolitan Magistrate Court, Saidapet, seeking to punish J. Jayalalitha, respondent No. 1 herein, for offence under section 169, IPC for having purchased Government land in violation of Code of Conduct for Ministers. In view of several

---

1. AIR 2004 SC 960.
2. JT 1998 (3) SC 318.
3. AIR 2004 SC 692.

complaints and on the basis of media reports, the Government referred the matter to C.B.C.I.D. on which a case came to be registered in crime No. 17 of 1996". Ms. J. Jayalalitha was charged under section 120B, IPC, section 13(2) read with sections 13(1)(c) and 13(1)(d) of the Prevention of Corruption Act, and sections 409, 169 and 420 read with section 34, IPC.

The Supreme Court referred to the provisions of section 13(1)(c) and 13(1)(d) of the Prevention of Corruption Act, 1988 acquitted the accused of the charges under section 13(1)(c) and 13(1)(d). However, with respect to charges under section 405 of the Indian Penal Code (IPC), the Supreme Court held as under:—

> "Persons in public life are expected to maintain very high standards of probity and, particularly, when there is likely to be even least bit of conflict of interest between the office one holds and the acts to be done by such person, ought to desist himself from indulging in the same. Such standards of behaviour were scrupulously observed in the earlier days after independence, but those values have now dwindled and instances of persons holding high elective offices indulging in self-aggrandizement by utilising Government property or in distribution of the largesse of the Government to their own favourites or for certain *quid pro quo* are on the increase. We have to strongly condemn such actions. Good ethical behaviour on the part of those who are in power is the hallmark of a good administration and people in public service rather than by assuming power to indulge in callous cupidity regardless of self-imposed discipline".

The Court held that irrespective of the conclusion about the guilt of Ms. J. Jayalalitha's offence with which she was charged, she must atone for the same by answering her conscience by not only returning the property to TANSI unconditionally but also ponder over whether she had done the right thing in breaching the spirit of the Code of Conduct and given rise to suspicion that Rules and Procedures were bent to clear the public property for personal benefit. The Supreme Court thus reminded the Chief Minister and other high dignitaries of their moral responsibility, apart from the technicalities of the criminal laws.

In the case of *M.C. Mehta* v. *Union of India*,[1] in the famous Taj Heritage Corridor Project scam the Supreme Court directed the CBI to lodge FIR against officers and persons involved in the matter, and hold investigations against the Chief Minister of Uttar Pradesh (Ms. Mayavati, the Chief Minister of Uttar Pradesh).

---

1. AIR 2004 SC 800.

Another land mark judgment was delivered by a Bench of Justice H.K. Sema and Justice AR. Lakshmanan regarding allotment of residence to Justice B.P. Banerjee of the Kolkata High Court. The Apex Court in November 2004 cancelled the allotment of a plot made to Justice Banerjee in 1987 and ordered public auction of the house constructed by him on it. The Apex Court, while cancelling the allotment, had said: " Justice Banerjee has misused his divine judicial duty as liveries to accomplish his personal ends. He has betrayed the trust reposed on him by the people. To say the least, this is bad. There is nothing wrong in a Judge to have ambition to achieve something, but if the ambition to achieve is likely to cause compromise with his divine judicial duty, better not to pursue it." Justice Banerjee in an interim application challenged the auction on the ground that it was not done properly.

Rejecting his application, the Bench deprecated the filing of such applications and described it as an attempt to circumvent its order. The Bench also directed the Registry not to accept any such interim applications without its prior permission. The case was reported in Hindu dated 11-3-2006.

The Supreme Court in another land mark judgment reported in The Tribune, Chandigarh dated 21-4-2008, the Apex Court has upheld the conviction of a Hyderabad Sessions Judge on charge of bribery after being let off by the A.P. High Court.

Upholding the award of three years' rigorous imprisonment to D. Janardhana Rao in 1996 case for taking a bribe of Rs. 4 lakh in a case pending before him and promising the accused that they would be acquitted if they paid the money, a Bench of Justice B.N. Agrawal and Mr. Justice A.K. Mathur said, "the High Court was wholly unjustified in doubting the veracity" of the evidence of witnesses against the judge, Mr. Rao, at that time, was IIIrd Metropolitan Sessions Judge of Hyderabad. ".............the judgment of the High Court acquitting him suffers from the vice of perversity as it has refused to place reliance upon the evidence of witness merely on the basis of certain minor contradictions in their evidences, though they have supported the prosecution case on all material particulars," the Apex Court ruled.

The Bench also took exception to the High Court making certain adverse remarks against the then Registrar (Vigilance) of the High Court for granting permission for prosecution of Mr. Rao and ordered expunging of the same from the records.

It will thus be seen that the Supreme Court has not spared a Sessions Judge, who was awarded sentence of imprisonment for taking bribe in a case pending before him. The Supreme Court is quite alive to stop the corruption by persons holding high public positions and reminding them of the moral duties they owe to the society.

Part IV

Law and Human Rights

LAW AND HUMAN RIGHTS

DISCRIMINATION AGAINST WOMEN-VIOLATION OF HUMAN RIGHTS

The call for gender justice, and discrimination against women has become very important at the present juncture. Discrimination against women has been a burning issue during this century, and the subject-matter of hot debate not only in this country but also all over the world. It is necessary to examine the phenomenon of discrimination against women as a violation of human rights.

Reference may be made to the Charter of the United Nations, wherein the people of the United Nations reaffirmed faith in fundamental human rights, in the dignity and worth of the human persons, in the equal rights of men and women and of nations large and small, and to establish conditions under which justice and respect for the obligations arising from treaties and other sources of international law could be maintained.

Reference may also be made to the following purpose and principles enunciated in article (I), particularly providing:—

> "...........to achieve international co-operation in solving international problems of an economic, social, cultural or humanitarian character, and in promoting and encouraging respect for human rights and for fundamental freedoms for all without distinction as to race, sex, language or religion".

Reference may also be made to the Universal Declaration of Human Rights, 1948, which provides for a common standard of achievement for all peoples and all nations, to the end that every individual and every organ of society will keep this Declaration constantly in mind.

The Universal Declaration of Human Rights is one of the most important documents of this century, which has inspired and influenced nations all over the world. It has been a source of inspiration for the entire mankind. It was on the night of 10th December, 1948, that the General Assembly of United Nations adopted and proclaimed without a dissenting vote the Universal Declaration of Human Rights. The concept of Human Rights is a worldwide one stretching over a long period of history. Its history starts from the *Magna Carta* of the 13th Century and continues upto the present century throughout the length and breadth of the world.

Reference may be made to article 2 which is given below:—

> "Everyone is entitled to all the rights and freedoms set forth in this Declaration, without distinction of any kind, such as race, colour, sex, language, religion, political or other opinion, national or social origin, birth or other status".

It will be abundantly clear that human rights clearly provide for equal rights and freedoms without any distinction of any kind based on race, colour or sex. The various articles referred to in the said Declaration equally apply to men and women.

Reference in this connection is necessary to be made to the convention on the "Elimination of all foms of discrimination against women 1979".

The above Convention was adopted by the United Nations on December 18, 1979. The Convention provides an international standard for protecting and promoting women's human rights and is often referred to as a "Bill of Rights" for women. It establishes a minimum set of standards for combating discrimination against women. It is the only international instrument that comprehensively addresses itself to women's rights political, civil, cultural, economic and social. As on July 2002, 170 countries had ratified the Women's Convention. In the nations that have ratified the treaty, CEDAW has provided invaluable inputs in reducing the effects of discrimination against women, which include violence, poverty and lack of legal protection along with the denial of inheritance, property rights and access to credit. India ratified the Convention on the Elimination of All Forms of Discrimination Against Women on 25-6-1993. It is necessary to refer to some details of the said important and far reaching Convention. The Convention noted that the Charter of the United Nations reaffirms faith in fundamental human rights, in the dignity and worth of the human person and in the equal rights of men and women, and further stated that the Universal Declaration of Human Rights affirms the principle of the inadmissibility of discrimination and proclaims that all human beings are born free and equal in dignity and rights and that everyone is entitled to all the rights and freedoms set forth therein, without distinction of any kind, including distinction based on sex.

The Convention further noticed that the States that are party to the International Covenants on Human Rights have the obligation to ensure equal right of men and women to enjoy all economic, social, cultural, civil and political rights.

The Convention further recalled that discrimination against women violates the principles of equality of rights and respect for human dignity, is an obstacle to the participation of women, on equal terms with men, in the political, social, economic and cultural life of their countries. It hampers the growth of the prosperity of the society and the family and makes the full development of the potentialities of women in the service of their countries and of humanity more difficult.

In all there are 30 articles in the said Convention. Reference may only be made to a few of them.

Article 2: Article 2 provides that the States Parties condemn discrimination against women in all its forms, agree to pursue by all appropriate means and without delay a policy of eliminating discrimination against women. The said article contains various undertakings to achieve the said objective in clauses (a) to (g).

Article 3: Article 3 provides that States Parties shall take in all fields, in particular in the political, socio economic and cultural fields, all appropriate measures, including legislation, to ensure full development and advancement of women, for the purpose of guaranteeing them the exercise and enjoyment of human rights and fundamental freedoms on a basis of equality with men.

Article 6: Article 6 provides that States Parties shall take all appropriate measures, including legislation, to suppress all forms of traffic in women and their sexual exploitation.

Article 7: Article 7 provides for taking appropriate measures to eliminate discrimination against women in the political and public life of the country and to ensure equality to the women.

Article 10: Article 10 provides that States Parties shall take all appropriate measures to eliminate discrimination against women in order to ensure to them equal rights with men in the field of education, and give details of the same.

Article 11: Article 11 provides that States Parties shall take all appropriate measures to eliminate discrimination against women in the field of employment in order to ensure, on a basis of equality of men and women, the same rights, and provide illustrations of the same.

Article 12: Article 12 provides that States Parties shall take all appropriate measures to eliminate discrimination against women in the field of health care in order to ensure, on a basis of equality of men and women, access to health care services, including those related to family planning.

Article 13: Article 13 provides that States Parties shall take all appropriate measures to eliminate discrimination against women in other areas of economic and social life in order to ensure, on a basis of equality of men and women, the same rights, which have been further elaborated.

Article 14: Article 14 deals with problems of rural women and similarly provides that States Parties shall take all appropriate measures to eliminate discrimination against women in rural areas in order to ensure, on a basis of equality of men and women, that they participate in and benefit from rural development, and give various examples of the same.

Article 15: Article 15 accords to the women equality with men before law, equality in civil matters, in all contracts and in relation to law relating to the movement of persons and the freedom to choose their residence and domicile.

Article 16: Article 16 provides that States Parties shall take all appropriate measures to eliminate discrimination against women in all matters relating to marriage and family relations, and provide illustrations of the same.

Article 17: Article 17 provides for the implementation of the present Convention by establishing a Committee on the elimination of Discrimination Against Women and other procedural matters relating thereto.

Article 24: Article 24 provides that States Parties undertake to adopt all necessary measures at the national level aimed at achieving full realization of the rights recognized in the present Convention.

Article 30: Article 30 provides that the authentic texts of the Convention in various languages *viz.* Arabic, Chinese, English, French, Russian and Spanish shall be deposited with the Secretary-General of the United Nations.

Reference may also be made to the Beijing Declaration, Fourth World Conference on Women, 1995, which under clause 14, specifically provides equal rights, opportunities and access to resources, equal sharing of responsibilities for the family by men and women, and a harmonious partnership between them are critical to their well being and that of their families as well as to the consolidation of democracy.

Reference may also be made to the following Articles:

Article 23: Article 23 ensures the full enjoyment by women and the girl child of all human rights and fundamental freedoms and takes effective action against violations of these rights and freedoms.

Article 24: Article 24 takes all necessary measures to eliminate all forms of discrimination against women and the girl child and removes all obstacles to gender equality and the advancement and empowerment of women.

Article 26: Article 26 promotes women's economic independence, including employment, and eradicates the persistent and increasing burden of poverty on women, by addressing the structural cause of poverty through changes in economic structures, ensuring equal access for all women, including those in rural areas, as vital development agents, to productive resources, opportunities and public services.

Article 29: Article 29 prevents and eliminates all forms of violence against women and girls.

Article 31: Article 31 promotes and protects all human rights of women and girls.

Article 34: Article 34 relates to the development of the potential of girls and women of all ages so as to ensure their full and equal participation in building a better world for all and to enhance their role in the development process.

It will be, thus, seen that as far as the international law is concerned, the women, which includes girls, have been guaranteed equal treatment, and the same assures the elimination of all forms of discrimination against women.

The case of sexual violation against women came up for hearing before the Supreme Court in case *State of Himachal Pradesh* v. *Shree Kant Shekari*.[1] The Supreme Court held as under:—

> "Sexual violence apart from the being a dehumanizing act is an unlawful intrusion on the right of privacy and sanctity of a female. It is a serous blow to her supreme honour and offences herself-esteem and dignity it degrades and humiliates the victim and where

1. AIR 2004 SC 4404.

the victim is a helpless innocent child or a minor, it leaves behind a traumatic experience. A rapist not only causes physical injuries but more indelibly leaves a scar on the most cherished possession of a woman *i.e.* her dignity, honour, reputation and not the least her chastity. Rape is not only a crime against the person of a woman, it is a crime against the entire society."

The Supreme Court referred to its earlier decision in *Bothisattwa Gautam* v. *Subhra Chakraborty*[1] in the following manner:—

"It is a crime against basic human rights, and is also violative of the victim's most cherished of the Fundamental Rights, namely, the Right to Life contained in article 21 of the Constitution of India, 1950 (in short the 'Constitution') the Courts, are therefore, expected to deal with cases of sexual crime against women with utmost sensitivity. Such cases need to be dealt with sternly and severely."

Mr. Justice S.B. Sinha, Judge Supreme Court of India in his article "Women and Human Rights" published in the Human Rights Year Book-2008 has dealt with in the following manner:—

"At the same time, even in the face of this stark reality, it cannot be denied that the judiciary has often preempted legislation in areas where declaration of rights and protection of interests are deeply needed. The judiciary has been staunch in its punishments of rapists and perpetrators of domestic violence and dowry harassment. They have come down heavily on discrimination of women in all fields. The judiciary has truly strived to protect the rights to life, liberty and security to the Indian women. Perhaps when this is achieved more can be accorded to efforts aimed to bring about altitudinal changes and holistic development of Indian women.

However, I would like to end the article with the following observations made by Noeleen Heyzer, Executive Director of the United Nations Development Fund for Women made on "Women's Day" on 8th March, 2005, she observed thus:

"Thirty years after the beginning of the Decade of Women, and 10 years after Beijing, it is still a woman's face we see when we speak of poverty, of HIV/AIDS, of violent conflict and social upheaval, of trafficking in human beings...."

---

1. AIR 1996 SC 922.

HUMAN RIGHTS DEVELOPMENT AND DEMOCRATISATION*

The Universal Declaration of Human Rights is one of the most important documents of this century and has inspired and influenced nations all over the world. It has been a source of inspiration for the entire mankind. It was on the night of 10th December, 1948, that the General Assembly of United Nations adopted and proclaimed without a dissenting vote the Universal Declaration of Human Rights. The concept of Human Rights is a world-wide one stretching over a long period of history.

Its history starts from the *Magna Carta* of the 13th Century and continues up to the present century throughout the length and breadth of the world.

Reference may also be made to the British Bill of Rights 1688, French Declaration of Bill of Rights of the Man and Citizens (1789), the Bill of Rights of the United States of America (1791) and even to the Constitution of the USSR (1936).

A new dimension has been added to the concept and it is now realised that the protection of human rights was not necessarily the concern of the people of different States where those rights were violated but that it was the concern of the whole of mankind to ensure the preservation and promotion of human rights in all parts of the world. The Charter of the United Nations which was adopted after the war gave prominence to the aim of promoting human rights and freedoms. In the Preamble of the Charter it was proclaimed, "We, the people of United Nations determined... to reaffirm faith in fundamental human rights, dignity and birth of human person, in the equal rights of men and women and of nations, large and small ... have resolved to combine our efforts to accomplish these aims". In the very first article of the charter one of the declared purposes of the United Nations was the achievement of international co-operation in promoting and encouraging respect for

---

* A paper published by The Law Association for Asia and the Pacific, 13th and 16th September, 1993.

human rights. Article 68 of the Charter provided for setting up of several Commissions including one for the promotion of human rights. Accordingly, the Commission of Human Rights was duly constituted in 1946. The draft declaration of human rights was submitted to the General Assembly of the United Nations in September, 1948 and the Universal Declaration of Human Rights was adopted by the General Assembly on 10th of December, that year. The Universal Declaration of Human Rights was adopted by the General Assembly as a "common standard of achievement for all people and nations". The declaration of human rights has acquired a degree of authority, and it has virtually become a part of international law:

In India the essential human rights have been embodied in those parts of the Constitution which deal with fundamental rights and directive principles of State policy.

The Universal Declaration of Human Rights starts with a Preamble and proclaims human rights as a common standard of achievement for all people and all nations. There are 30 articles in the Universal Declaration of Human Rights.

I would like to refer to some of the salient articles of the Universal Declaration of Human Rights.

Article 1

All human beings are born free and equal in dignity and rights. They are endowed with reason and conscience and should act towards one another in a spirit of brotherhood.

Article 2

Everyone is entitled to all the rights and freedoms set forth in this Declaration, without distinction of any kind, such as race, colour, sex, language, religion, political or other opinion, national or social origin, property, birth or other status.

Furthermore, no distinction shall be made on the basis of the political, jurisdictional or international status of the country or territory to which a person belongs, whether it be independent, trust, non-self-governing or under any other limitation of sovereignty.

Article 3

Everyone has the right to life, liberty and security of person.

Article 7

All are equal before the law and are entitled without any discrimination to equal protection of the law. All are entitled to equal protection against any discrimination in violation of this Declaration and against any incitement to such discrimination.

Article 13

1. Everyone has the right to freedom of movement and residence within the borders of each State.

2. Everyone has the right to leave any country, including his own, and to return to his country.

Article 17

1. Everyone has the right to own property alone as well as in association with others.

2. No one shall be arbitrarily deprived of his property.

Article 18

Everyone has the right to freedom of thought, conscience and religion; this right includes freedom to change his religion or belief, and freedom, either alone or in community with others and in public or private, to mainfest his religion or belief in teaching, practice, worship and observance.

Article 19

Everyone has the right to freedom of opinion and expression; this right includes freedom to hold opinions without interference and to seek, receive and impart information and ideas through any media and regardless of frontiers.

Article 20

1. Everyone has the right to freedom of peaceful assembly and association.

2. No one may be compelled to belong to an association.

Article 23

1. Everyone has the right to work, to free choice of employment, to just and favourable conditions of work and to protection against unemployment.

2. Everyone, without any discrimination, has the right to equal pay for equal work.

3. Everyone who works has the right to just and favourable remuneration ensuring for himself and his family an existence worthy of human dignity, and supplemented, if necessary by other means of social protection.

4. Everyone has the right to form and to join trade unions for the protection of his interests.

Article 26

1. Everyone has the right to education. Education shall be free, at least in the elementary and fundamental stages. Elementary education shall be compulsory. Technical and professional education shall be made generally available and higher education shall be equally accessible to all on the basis of merit.

2. Education shall be directed to the full development of the human personality and to the strengthening of respect for human rights and fundamental freedoms. It shall promote understanding, tolerance and friendship among all nations, racial or religious groups, and shall further the activities of the United Nations for the maintenance of peace.

3. Parents have a prior right to choose the kind of education that shall be given to their children.

Article 30

Nothing in this Declaration may be interpreted as implying for any State, group or person any right to engage in any activity or to perform any act aimed at the destruction of any of the rights and freedoms set forth herein.

There is a strong resemblance between the rights guaranteed under the Indian Constitution and the Declaration of Human Rights for instance articles 14 to 18 of the Constitution of India which guaranteed "Right to Equality" are similar to the provision of articles 1 and 7 of the Declaration of Human Rights. Article 3 of the Declaration has similarity with article 21 of the Constitution of India which guarantees protection of life and personal liberty. Article 4 of the Declaration is similar to articles 23 and 24 of the Indian Constitution which guaranteed right against exploitation and articles 22 and 27 of the Declaration are similar to the provisions of articles 29 and 30 of the Constitution of India which guarantees Right to Freedom of Religion. Article 17 of the Declaration corresponded to article 31 of the Indian Constitution. Similarly articles 13, 17, 18, 19, 20 and 23 of the Declaration correspond to article 19 of the Indian Constitution, which guaranteed Cultural and Educational Rights. It is no wonder that the Supreme Court of India has dealt with not only the rights guaranteed under the Indian Constitution but specifically also with the Rights enshrined under the Declaration of Human Rights. In this, the importance of the Universal Declaration of Human Rights has been emphasised by the Supreme Court of India in various judgments and reference may be made to some of the leading Indian judgments in this context. Reference can be made to the following important decisions of the Indian Supreme Court.

1. *Maneka Gandhi* v. *Union of India*;[1]
2. *M.H. Hoskot* v. *State of Maharashtra*;[2]
3. *Hussainara Khatoon* v. *Home Secretary*;[3]
4. *Randhir Singh* v. *Union of India*;[4]
5. *Kishore Chand* v. *State of Himachal Pradesh*;[5]

In the case of *M.H. Hoskot* v. *State of Maharashtra*,[6] it has been emphasised that the Indian socio-legal milieu makes free legal service, at trial and higher levels, an imperative processual pieces of criminal justice where deprivation of life or personal liberty hangs in the judicial balance. Reference was also made to article 8 of the Universal Declaration of Human Rights in this important judgment of the Supreme Court of India. In this case various directions were issued in respect of persons who are sentenced to prison.

The case of *Maneka Gandhi* v. *Union of India*,[7] was heard by a Constitution Bench of the Supreme Court of India. In this case the Petitioner's passport was impounded in public interest and the Government of India declined in the interest of the general public to further the reasons for the decision and the Petitioner filed the Writ Petition under article 32 of the Constitution of India to challenge the order.

It was held that article 21 of the Constitution is also a recognition of the Declaration of Rights which inhere in every individual.

It was held in this case that right to go abroad is a right included in personal liberty within article 21 and thus a fundamental right is affected by the impounding.

It was specifically noted in the judgment that only a shortwhile before the Indian Constitution came into force, the constitutional debate was still going on and the Universal Declaration of Human Rights was adopted by the General Assembly of the United Nations on 10th December, 1948. And most of the fundamental rights which we find included in Part III were recognised and adopted by the United Nations as the inalienable rights of man in the Universal Declaration of Human Rights. Article 13 of the Universal Declaration declared that "every one has a right to freedom of opinion and expression, this right includes freedom to hold opinions

1. (1978) 2 SCR 621.
2. (1979) 1 SCR 192.
3. (1979) 3 SCR 169.
4. (1982) 3 SCR 298.
5. (1991) 1 SCC 286.
6. AIR 1978 SC 1548: (1978) Cr LJ 1678: (1979) 1 SCR 192.
7. (1978) 2 SCR 621.

without interference and to seek, receive and import information and ideas through any media and regardless of frontiers". This was the glorious declaration of the fundamental freedom of speech and expression in conception and in scope. It was before the Constitution makers when they enacted article 19(1)(a). We have, therefore, no doubt that freedom of speech and expression guaranteed by article 19(1)(a) is exercisable not only in India but also outside, the Court ruled.

In the case of *Hussainara Khatoon* v. *State of Bihar*,[1] it was held that speedy trial for determination of the guilt is an integral and essential part of the fundamental right to life, particularly enshrined in article 21.

In the case of *Francis Coralie* v. *Union Territory of Delhi*,[2] it was held that the right of detainee to consult a legal adviser of his choice for any purpose not necessarily limited to defence in a criminal proceeding but also for securing release from preventive detention or filing a writ petition or prosecuting any claim or proceeding, civil or criminal, is obviously included in the right to live with human dignity and is also a part of the personal liberty and the detainee cannot be deprived of his right nor can this right of the detainee be interfered with except in accordance with reasonable, fair and just procedure established by a valid law.

It will thus be seen that the Supreme Court of India has been a pioneer in defending the violation of Human Rights anywhere. The Supreme Court has been the defender and protector of not only the Constitutional rights guaranteed under the Indian Constitution but also the human rights guaranteed by the Universal Declaration of Human Rights.

In one of the recent decisions of the Supreme Court of India in the case of *Unnikrishnan, J.P.* v. *State of Andhra Pradesh*,[3] which is known as the capitation fee case the Supreme Court held that right to education is a part of the right to life and the learned Judge relied on article 26(1) of the Universal Declaration of Human Rights.

These decisions are landmark decisions which show the extreme importance in which the Supreme Court of India holds the Universal Declaration of Human Rights. The development of Human Rights is extending into new horizon, for example the scope of the Human Rights is extending to human environment, meeting the menace of armed terrorist groups in different parts of the world in furtherance of alleged political causes, fighting the menace of international drug trafficking and

1. (1979) 3 SCR 169.
2. (1981) 1 SCC 608: AIR 1981 SC 746.
3. (1993) 1 SCC 645.

even fighting the colonialism regimes which are still persisting in denying the basic and civil political rights to millions of helpless people. Thus, the scope of the Human Rights is indeed a panoramic one and stands widely expanded. It does not only cover the basic civil and political rights but also wide range of new rights which are socio-economic in nature and other rights, which are necessary for the enjoyment of the Human Rights. As pointed out by Shri P.P. Rao in a paper presented to the International Conference of Lawyers held on February 21, 1993 at New Delhi:

> "Creating a world free from colonial domination, free from wars and nuclear weapons, free from terrorism and communal clashes, free from environmental pollution and ecological imbalances, free from poverty and illiteracy, free from famine and epidemics and in short, free from fear and want is a difficult task. The pre-requisites for the enjoyment of human rights can be secured only by promotion of universal respect for human rights, organised public opinion and sustained work by States and citizens alike".

In an international workshop of Human Rights Subhash C. Pratap of Andhra Pradesh in his keynote address pointed out as under:

> "The human rights movement need to be further activated and made more intensive. Today, as never before, this movement needs all-round support of the free world, of the institutions, of the free world of lawyers and judges and of enlightened citizens and human rights activists. The unwritten code of Human Rights is the unwritten *Magna Carta* of all mankind".

Mr. Justice S.H. Kapadia, President, International Institute of Human Rights Society and presently Chief Justice of India in his article published in the Human Right Year Book 2009 has pointed out the special features of human rights in the following manner:

> "The source of Human Rights is man's moral nature (loosely called Human Nature). Human needs establishes Human Rights.
>
> Human Rights are needed not for life but for life with dignity. They shape political society. Human Rights jurisprudence is a mechanism to attain human dignity.
>
> Human Rights are based on the philosophy of value. They are not absolute. They are not unchanging. The basic feature of Human Rights is universality.
>
> Human rights is a mechanism. Human Rights provide the legal mandate to fulfil human needs. Therefore, Human Rights are the bedrock of social justice. Human rights mirror the social

> environmental context of the time Human Rights mirror values that have crystallized into rights, often embedded in constitutions/other ethical codes of conduct serving as guiding principles for a way of life. These values mirror a certain amount of complexity of philosophical, psychological, sociological and other variables".

Mr. Justice S. Mohan, former Judge Supreme Court of India in his article "Expanding Horizon of Human Rights" published in the Human Rights Year Book 2009 has dealt with the terrorism in the following manner:—

> "The existence and validity of Human Rights are not written in the stars. Those ideals and convictions, which resulted from historical experience, from the craving for beauty and harmony, have been readily accepted in theory by man and at all times have been trampled upon by the same people under the pressures of their animal instincts.
>
> A large part of history is therefore replete with the struggle for those Human Rights an eternal struggle in which a final victory can never be won. But to tire in that struggle would mean the ruin of society."

It is with this note I would like to close the present article.

CUSTODIAL CRIMES AND HUMAN RIGHTS VIOLATION

The topic of custodial crimes is relevant and important in the new millennium. Everyday the news of custodial crimes is one of the front line news in the National Newspapers. As pointed out in a recent decision of the Supreme Court, reported in *Abdul Gaffar Khan* v. *Vasant Raghunath Dhoble*,[1] "if it is assuming alarming proportions, now-a-days, all around it is merely on account of the devilish devices adopted by those at the helm of affairs who proclaim from roof tops to be the defenders of democracy and protectors of peoples' rights and yet do not hesitate to condescend behind the screen to let loose their men in uniform to settle personal scores, feigning ignorance of what happens and pretending to be peace loving puritans and saviours of citizens' rights".

Reference may be made to the observations of Justice Brandies, which have become classic and are in the following immortal words:—

"Government as the *omnipotent* and *omnipresent* teacher teaches the whole people by its example, if the Government becomes a law breaker, it breeds contempt for law, it invites every man to become a law into himself" [in (1928) 277 US 438, quoted in (1961) 367 US 643 (659)].

Reference may be made to the following observations of the Supreme Court judgment in the above referred case[1]:—

> "The diabolic recurrence of police torture resulting in a terrible scare in the minds of common citizens that their lives and liberty are under a new and unwarranted peril because guardians of law destroy the human rights by custodial violence and torture and invariably resulting in death. The vulnerability of human rights assumes a traumatic torture when functionaries of the State whose paramount duty is to protect the citizens and not to commit gruesome offences against them, in reality perpetrate them".

Custodial violence, torture and abuse of police power are not peculiar to this country, but it is widespread. It has been the concern of

1. (2003) 7 SCC 749.

international community because the problem is universal and the challenge is almost global. The Universal Declaration of Human Rights was adopted by the General Assembly on 10th December, 1948[1] as "a common standard of achievement for all people and nations". The Universal Declaration of Human Rights has acquired a degree of authority, and it has virtually become a part of international law. In India the essential human rights have been embodied in those parts of the Constitution which deal with fundamental rights and directive principles of State Policy.

The Universal Declaration of Human Rights starts with a Preamble and proclaims the human rights as a common standard of achievement for all people and all nations. There are 30 articles in the Universal Declaration of Human Rights. In this article the human rights are relevant only as far as the custodial crimes are concerned and articles 3, 5, 8, 9, 13 are directly relevant and attracted. Articles 3, 5, 8, 9 and 13 are readily recapitulated, for easy reference.

Article 3: Every one has the right to life, liberty and security of person.

Article 5: No one shall be subjected to torture or to cruel inhuman or degrading treatment or punishment.

Article 8: Every one has the right to an effective remedy to the competent national tribunals for acts violating the fundamental rights granted to him by the Constitution or by law.

Article 9: No one shall be subjected to arbitrary arrest, detention or exile.

Article 13: Every one has the right to freedom of movement and residence within the borders of each State. Every one has the right to leave any country, including his own, and to return to his country.

The readers will immediately notice the resemblance between these and the Fundamental rights guaranteed under Part III of the Constitution of India.[2] The relevant ones, for this article are noted below:—

Protection of certain rights regarding freedom of speech, etc. article 19(1)—All citizens shall have the right—

(a) to freedom of speech and expression;

(b) to assemble peacefully and without arms;

---

1. Universal Declaration of Human Rights, 1948.
2. Constitution of India.

(c) to form associations or unions;

(d) to move freely throughout the territory of India;

(e) to reside and settle in any part of the territory of India; and

(f) to practice and profession or to carry on any occupation, trade or business.

Article 20(3): No person accused of any offence shall be compelled to be a witness against himself.

Article 21: Protection of life and personal liberty: No person shall be deprived of his life or personal liberty except according to procedure established by law.

Article 22: Protection against arrest and detention in certain cases—

(i) No person who is arrested shall be detained in custody without being informed as soon as may be, of the grounds for such arrest nor shall he be denied the right to consult, and to be defended by, a legal practitioner of his choice.

(ii) Every person who is arrested and detained in custody shall be produced before the nearest Magistrate within a period of twenty-four hours of such arrest excluding the time necessary for the journey from the place of arrest to the court of the Magistrate and no such person shall be detained in custody beyond the said period without the authority of a Magistrate.

Article 32: Remedies for enforcement of rights conferred by this part:—

(i) The right to move the Supreme Court by appropriate proceedings for the enforcement of the rights conferred by this part is guaranteed.

(ii) The Supreme Court shall have power to issue directions or orders or writs, including writs in the nature of *habeas corpus, mandamus,* prohibition, *quo warranto* and *certiorari,* whichever may be appropriate, for the enforcement of any of the rights conferred by this part.

Now we come to examine the same for their interaction on custodial crimes which have been very much in the news in the recent days. Right from the days of British rule there has been a general mistrust of the police powers particularly in cases of police custody. Even a mere look at the Evidence Act[1] which was enacted in the year 1872, shows the total

1. Indian Evidence Act, 1872.

mistrust of the statements, etc., recorded in police custody. Section 25 itself provides that no confession made to a police officer shall be proved as against a person accused of any offence. Similarly section 26 provides that confession by an accused while in custody of police shall not be proved against him, unless it is made in the immediate presence of a Magistrate. The procedure providing for arrest of persons who are accused of committing an offence are provided in Chapter V of the Code of Criminal Procedure, 1973[1] and the powers of the police to investigate offence is provided under Chapter XII of the same. These powers are well-known to the readers and it is not necessary to recapitulate them for the purpose of this Article. Section 41 provides for the police officer to arrest in certain cases persons without an order from a Magistrate. The persons arrested cannot be detained by the police officers in custody for more than 24 hours without order of a Magistrate under section 167. The powers of arrest, being of a serious nature, have to be exercised under the Criminal Procedure Code. Similarly the powers of the police to investigate the offence has to be exercised only as per the provision prescribed under Chapter XII of the Criminal Procedure Code. The recording of confession, etc., has to be done strictly as prescribed under section 164. Similarly the search by police officers has to be conducted as prescribed under section 165 of the Criminal Procedure Code.

Having examined the legal provision let us have a look at the important decision of the Supreme Court in relation to the Custodial Crimes.

The question of arrest and detention of judicial officers has come in the most sensational case of arrest of the Chief Judicial Magistrate, Nadiad. The case become historic and is now reported in *Delhi Judicial Service Association* v. *State of Gujarat*.[2] The Supreme Court has dealt with the role of the police and has condemned the arbitrary and excessive use of force by the police. The judgment has salutary bearing to the custodial crime and the human rights. I would quote one passage from the said judgment.

"The main objective of police is to apprehend offenders, to investigate crimes and to prosecute them before the courts and also to prevent commission of crime and above all to ensure law and order to protect the citizen's life and property. The law enjoins the police to be scrupulously fair to the offender and the Magistracy is to ensure fair investigation and fair trial to an offender. The purpose and object of Magistracy and Police are complementary to each other. It is unfortunate, that these objectives

1. Code of Criminal Procedure, 1973.
2. JT 1991 (3) SC 617.

have remained unfulfilled even after 40 years of our Constitution. Aberrations of Police Officers and Police excesses in dealing with the law and order situation have been the subject of adverse comments from this Court as well as from other courts but it has failed to have any corrective effect on it. The police has power to arrest a person even without obtaining warrant of arrest from a court. The amplitude of this power casts an obligation on the police to take maximum care in exercising the power. The police must bear in mind, as held by this Court and if a person is arrested for a crime, his constitutional and fundamental rights must not be violated." See: *Sunil Batra* v. *Delhi Administration.*[1]

The extent of powers of police interrogation under section 161 of the Criminal Procedure Code *qua* the provision of article 20(3) of the Constitution of India came up for decision before the Supreme Court in the case of *Nandini Satpati* v. *P.L. Dani.*[2] The Court has given a lengthy judgment dealing with entire parameter of section 161(2) of the Criminal Procedure Code and in the light of the constitutional provisions it has been ultimately further held that the accused has a right to consult his lawyer under circumstances of near custodial interrogation, and it has been held that a lawyer's presence is a constitutional claim in some circumstances in our country also. The other useful observations of eminent writers and commentators on the powers of police during the investigation, are referred to and this is a landmark judgment.

In *Prem Shankar Shukla's* case,[3] the Supreme Court considered the question of placing a prisoner under handcuffs by the police. The Court declared that no prisoner shall be handcuffed or fettered routinely or merely for the convenience of custody or escort. The Court emphasized that the police did not enjoy any unrestricted or unlimited power to handcuff an arrested person. If having regard to the circumstances including the conduct, behaviour and character of a prisoner, there is reasonable apprehension of prisoner's escape from custody or disturbance of peace by violence, the police may put the prisoner under handcuff. If a prisoner is handcuffed without there being any justification, it would violate the prisoner's fundamental rights under articles 14 and 19 of the Constitution. To be consistent with articles 14 and 19 handcuffs must be the last refuge as there are other ways for ensuring security of a prisoner. In *Prem Shankar Shukla's* case, Krishna Iyer, J. observed—

> "................if today freedom of the forlorn person falls to the police somewhere tomorrow the freedom of many may fall, elsewhere,

1. AIR 1978 SC 1675: (1978) Cr LJ 1741.
2. AIR 1978 SC 1025.
3. AIR 1980 SC 1535: (1980) Cr LJ 930: (1980) 3 SCC 526.

with none to whimper unless the court process invigilates in time and polices, the police before it is too late".

One of the earlier leading cases of police torture is the case of *Rakesh Kaushik* v. *B.L. Vij, Superintendent, Central Jail, New Delhi.*[1] In that case a quasi *Habeas Corpus* petition was filed by a prisoner of Delhi Central Jail bitterly complaining with facts and figures of the terror and horror physical and psychic let loose on him and other jail inmates by a cryptocrimial combination of senior officers and superior prisoners. The Hon'ble Supreme Court ordered judicial inquiry by the District and Sessions Judge.

In other case which involved the arrest of an MLA while proceeding to attend the session of the Legislative Assembly, the Supreme Court in the case of *Bhim Singh* v. *State of Jamu & Kashmir,*[2] stated as under:—

> "We do not wish to use stronger words to condemn the authoritarian acts of the police. If the personal liberty of a Member of the Legislative Assembly is to be played with in this fashion, one can only wonder what may happen to lesser mortals. Police Officers who are the custodians of law and order should have the greatest respect for the personal liberty of citizens and should not flout the laws by stooping to such bizarre acts of lawlessness. Custodians of law and order should not become deprecators of civil liberties. Their duty is to protect and not to abduct."

It may be useful to make a very brief reference to other judgments of the Supreme Court, as the latest case law indicates specific and necessary guidelines necessary to be observed on the subject. In the case of *Gauri Shanker Sharma* v. *State of Uttar Pradesh,*[3] which was a case of a death in police custody, this is what the Supreme Court said, "This offence is of serious nature aggravated by the fact that it was committed by a person who is supposed to protect the citizens and not misuse his uniform and authority to brutally assault them seriously viewed for otherwise we will help take a stride in the direction of police raj. It must be curbed with a heavy hand. The punishment should be such as would deter others from indulging in such behaviour. There can be no room for leniency."

Reference may be made to the judgment of the Supreme Court in the case of *Nilabati Behera* v. *State of Orissa.*[4] In this case the admitted facts are:—

---

1. AIR 1981 SC 1767.
2. AIR 1986 SC 494: (1985) 4 SCC 677.
3. JT 1990 (1) SC 6.
4. AIR 1993 SC 1960.

> "The admitted facts are that Suman Behera was taken in police custody on 1-12-1987 at 8 A.M. and he was found dead the next day on the railway track near the Police Outpost Jeraikela, without being released from custody, and his death was unnatural, caused by the multiple injuries sustained by him".

The Supreme Court reached the conclusions recorded in a Joint Inquiry conducted by District Magistrate that it was a case of custodial death and Suman Behera died as a result of injury inflicted voluntarily while he was in police custody at the Police Station, Jeraikela. The Hon'ble Supreme Court made reference to its earlier decision in the case of *Rudul Sah* v. *State of Bihar*;[1] *Sebastian* v. *Union of India*,[2] and *Bhim Singh* v. *State of J&K*[3] and of *Saheli*.[4] The Court also referred to the case of *Union Carbide Corporation* v. *Union of India*,[5] and the Supreme Court held as under:—

> "Custodial death is perhaps one of the worst crimes in a civilized society governed by the Rules of Law. The rights inherent in articles 21 and 22(1) of the Constitution require to be jealously and scrupulously protected. We cannot whisk away the problem. Any form of torture or cruel, inhuman or degrading treatment would fall within the inhibition of article 21 of the Constitution, whether it occurs during investigation, interrogation or otherwise. If the functionaries of the Government become law breakers, it is bound to breed contempt for law and would encourage lawlessness and every man would have the tendency to become law unto himself thereby leading to anarchisim".

The Court also referred to article 9(5) of the international covenant on civil and political rights 1966 which indicates that an enforceable right to compensation is not alien to the concept of enforcement of guaranteed right.

Reference may also be made to a judgment of the Supreme Court, in the case of *D.K. Basu* v. *State of West Bengal*,[6] where *inter alia* it was held that—

> "No violation of any of the human rights has been the subject of so many Conventions and Declarations as 'torture'– all aiming at total banning of it in all forms, but inspite of the commitments made to eliminate torture, the fact remains that torture is more widespread

1. AIR 1983 SC 1086: (1983) 3 SCR 508.
2. (1984) 1 SCR 904.
3. (1985) 4 SCC 677.
4. (1990) 1 SCC 422.
5. (1991) 4 SCC 584.
6. AIR 1997 SC 610.

now than ever before. "Custodial torture" is a naked violation of human dignity and degradation which destroys, to a very large extent, the individual personality. It is a calculated assault on human dignity and whenever human dignity is wounded, civilisation takes a step backward-flag of humanity must on each such occasion fly half-mast".

In a very recent case, *Shakila Abdul Gafar Khan* v. *Vasant Raghunath Dhoble,*[1] although, the Supreme Court declined to interfere with the judgment of acquittal by the High Court yet considered the same to be a fit case for exercise of jurisdiction under article 142 of the Constitution and directed the State to pay a compensation of Rs. 1,00,000 to the mother and the children of the deceased. The Court also directed an enquiry to be conducted by the Head of the Police Force of the State under direct control of the Chief Secretary of the State to find out as to who were the persons responsible for the injury on the body of the deceased. It was also directed that action will also be taken against the officials who did not register FIR and the crime branch who were requested to conduct above authority of enquiry but did not appear to have done anything in the matter.

In a later case *Munshi Singh Gautam* v. *State of Madhya Pradesh.*[2] The question of custodial crimes, in relation to article 21, 20(3) and 22 of the Constitution of India came up for consideration.

The Supreme Court held as under:—

> "It is, therefore, difficult to comprehend how torture and custodial violence can be permitted to defy the rights flowing from the Constitution. The dehumanizing torture, assault and death in custody which have assumed alarming proportions raise serious questions about the credibility of rule of law and administration of criminal justice system. The community rightly gets disturbed. The cry for justice becomes louder and warrants immediate remedial measures".

The Supreme Court referred to observations of Mr. Justice Brandies which are as under:—

> "Government as the omnipotent and omnipresent teacher teaches the whole people by its example, if the Government becomes a law breaker, it breeds contempt for law, it invites every man to become a law into himself, in (1928) 277 US 438, quoted in (1961) 367 US 643 (659)."

1. (2003) 7 SCC 749.
2. AIR 2005 SC 402.

The Supreme Court further held as under:—

> "The diabolic recurrence of police torture resulting in a terrible scare in the minds of common citizens that their lives and liberty are under a new and unwarranted peril because guardians of law destroy the human rights by custodial violence and torture and invariably resulting in death. The vulnerability of human rights assumes a traumatic torture when functionaries of the State whose paramount duty is to protect the citizens and not to commit gruesome offences against them, in reality perpetrate them. It is the duty of the police, when a crime is reported, to collect evidence to be placed during trial to arrive at the truth. That certainly would not include torturing a person, be he an accused or a witness to extract information. The duty should be done within four corners of law. Law enforcers cannot take law into their hands in the name of collecting evidence."

It is not necessary to multiply references to the Court cases, it is sufficient to say that courts have taken a very serious note of any violation of human rights during the period when the persons are in police custody, and of a place of eminence is according to the human rights. I may end by saying that human rights are permanent, inalienable, undestructible, and are in the nature of beacon light, all pointing towards the goal of "one world".

RIO DECLARATION OF ENVIRONMENT PROTECTION AND SUBSEQUENT DEVELOPMENTS

"Since time immemorial, natural object like rivers enjoyed a high position in the life of the society. They were considered as Goddesses having not only the purifying capacity but also self purifying ability. Fouling of the water of a river was considered a sin and it attracted punishments of different grades which included, penance, outcasting, fine, etc. The earth or soil also equally had the same importance, and the ancient literature provided the means of purifying the polluted soil. The above are some of the many illustrations to support the view that environmental pollution was controlled rigidly in the ancient time. It was not an affair linked to an individual or individuals but the society as a whole accepted its duty to protect the environment. The 'dharma' of environment was to sustain and ensure progress and welfare of all. The inner urge of the individuals to follow the set norms of the society, motivated them to allow the natural objects to remain in the natural state. Apart from this motivation, there was the fear of punishment. There were efforts, not just to punish the culprit but to balance the ecosystems. The noteworthy development in this period was that each individual knew his duty to protect the environment and he tried to act accordingly".[1]

The unprecedented increase in the number and the activities of humans, since the industrial revolution particularly in this country, have given rise to a deterioration of the environment and depletion of natural resources that threaten the future of the planet.

It was in this background that a world conference was held at Stockholm in 1972[2] (from 6th to 16th June, 1972) to express concern on the depletion of resources in forest, mineral wealth, marine life and other natural wealth. It was also to share common concern on pollution of the air and water, deterioration in the status of world environment. It was stated in the proclamation in these profound words:

---

1. Law & Environment by P. Leela Krishnan referred to by the Supreme Court in *K.N. Chinnapa* v. *Union of India*, AIR 2003 SC 724.
2. World Conference Stockholm 1972.

"Man is both creature and moulder of his environment which gives his physical sustenance and affords him the opportunity for intellectual, moral, social and spiritual growth. In the long and tortuous evolution of the human race on this planet a stage has been reached when through the rapid acceleration of science and technology, man has acquired the power to transform his environment in countless ways and on an unprecedented scale. Both aspects of men's environment, the natural and the man made, are essential to his well being and to the enjoyment of basic human rights even the right to life itself."

The protection and improvement of the human environment is a major issue which affects the well being of people's economic development throughout the world, it is the urgent desire of the peoples of the whole world, and the duty of all Governments. It was at this conference that late Mrs. Indira Gandhi made the famous speech in which she stressed the need of linking environment with development at a global level. The conference was on human environment. The United Nations also appointed an environment commission, headed by Mrs. Gro Harlem Brundtland, Prime Minister of Norway. As pointed out by Maurice F. Strong, Secretary-General of the United Nations Conference on Environment and Development:[1]

"It is ironic that these impacts have occurred largely as a result of processes that have produced such unparalleled levels of wealth and prosperity in the industrialised world".

Great imbalance has been created by the concentration of economic growth in the industralised countries and population growth in developing countries and this is the key issue facing the world at the present juncture. The United Nations General Assembly adopted on October 29, 1982,[2] the World Charter for Nature. The charter declares the awareness that:

"(a) Mankind is a part of nature and life depends on the uninterrupted functioning of natural systems which ensure the supply of energy and nutrients.

(b) Civilisation is rooted in nature, which has shaped human culture and influenced all artistic and scientific achievement, and living in harmony with nature gives man the best opportunities for the development of his creativity, and for rest and recreation".

---

1. United Nations Conference on Environment & Development.
2. United Nations General Assembly Resolution October 29, 1982.

In December, 1989, the United Nations General Assembly, responding to the report of the Brundtland Commission, decided to hold a conference on environment and development in Rio de Jeneiro in June, 1992.[1] It was decided that nations will be represented at the United Nations Conference (UNCED) by their Heads of State or Government as a mark of importance to the issues involved.

June 14, 1992 will go down in the history of environmental protection as a landmark day. It was on this historic day that the Rio declaration on principles of general rights and obligations on environmental protection initiated by the Heads of the Government at the United Nations Conference on Environment and Development was settled.

The principles which are 27 in all recognise the interdependent nature of the earth and mark the beginning of a new era *viz.* that of environmental supremacy.

Principle No. 1 points that human beings are at the centre of the concerns for sustainable development and they are entitled to a healthy and productive life in harmony with nature.

Number of duties have been cast on the States, to employ their own resources pursuant to their own environmental policies and to ensure that activities within their jurisdiction or control do not cause damage to the environment of other States. This is what Principle No. 2 points out to (Principle No. 2).

Principle Nos. 3 and 4 deal with the right to development and show that the environmental protection and the right to development go hand in hand. Principle Nos. 3 and 4 are quoted below for easy reference:—

> "3. The right to development must be fulfilled so as to equitably meet developmental needs of present and future generations".
>
> "4. In order to achieve sustainable development, the environmental protection shall constitute an integral part of the development process and cannot be considered in isolation from it".

One of the important considerations concerns the need of the developing countries and States that the special situation and needs of developing countries, particularly the least developed and those most environmentally vulnerable, shall be given special priority. International actions in the field of environment and development should also address the interests and needs of all countries. (Principle No. 6).

Principle No. 8 points out that to achieve sustainable development and a higher quality of life for all people, States should reduce and

---

1. Rio De Jeneiro Conference June, 1992.

eliminate unsustainable patterns of production and consumption and promote appropriate demographic policies.

The citizens have an important role to play and environmental issues can only be best handled with the participation of all concerned citizens and that is the theme of Principle No. 10. At the national level each individual shall have the appropriate access to information concerning the environment which is available to the public authorities including information on hazardous materials and activities in their community.

States have been directed to enact effective environmental legislation. It also points out that the standards applied by some countries may be inappropriate and of unwarranted economic and social cost to the other countries in particular developing countries. (Principle No. 11).

The States have been enjoined to develop national law regarding liability and compensation for the victims of pollution and other environmental damage. The States are also enjoined to cooperate in an expeditious and in a more determined manner to develop further international law regarding liability and compensation for adverse effects of environmental damage caused by the activities within their jurisdiction or control to areas beyond their jurisdiction (Principle No. 13).

Principle No. 16 points out that the national authorities should take into account the approach that the polluter should, in principle bear the cost of pollution, with due regard to the public interest and without distorting international trade and investment.

Attention is also made to the vital role which women can play in environmental management and development. This is another landmark principle, which highlights an important role of women who constitute half of the mankind, and without whose co-operation, environmental protection would be incomplete. This is the theme of Principle No. 20.

The said declaration also points out that the importance of youth in environmental protection and the Principle No. 21 states that the creativity, ideals and courage of the youth of the world should be mobilised to forge a global partnership in order to achieve sustainable future for all.

The role of indigenous people and their communities has also been not lost sight of by the Rio Declaration. A duty is cast on the States to recognise and duly support their identity, culture and interests and enable their effective participation in the achievement of sustainable development. (Principle No. 22).

The Rio Declaration has also not lost sight of the environmental and natural resources of people under oppression, domination and occupation (Principle No. 23).

The destruction caused by warfare is the theme of Principle No. 24 and enjoins the States to respect international law providing protection for the environment in times of armed conflict. Peace and development are the key notes of Principle Nos. 25 and 26.

The last principle exhorts States and people to cooperate in good faith and in a spirit of partnership in the fulfilment of the principles embodied in this declaration and in the future development of international law in the field of sustainable development.

It is necessary to take note of subsequent development. The World Conference on Human Rights, held at Vienna in 1993, the Global Conference on the Sustainable Development of Small Island Developing States, held at Bridgetown, Barbados, in 1994 and the International Conference on Population and Development held at Cairo in 1994.

It is imperative to take notice of the Copenhagen Declaration which was adopted by the World Summit for Social Development held at Copenhagen[1] from 6th to 12th March, 1995. The various Heads of States and Governments assembled at Copenhagen at the invitation of the United Nations at the Summit meeting to recognise the significance of social development and human well being for all, and to give these guidelines, the highest priority both now and in the 21st century. The Conference shared the conviction that social development and social justice are indispensable for the achievement and maintenance of peace and security within and amongst the nations. The Conference was deeply convinced that economic development, social development and environmental protection are inter-dependent and mutually re-enforcing components for sustainable development which is the frame-work for the efforts to achieve a higher quality of life for all people.

The Conference was held on the eve of the 50th anniversary of the United Nations. The Conference reaffirmed that they were united by the Principle of the Charter of the United Nations and by various agreements reached at International Conference.

The questions of environmental protection have been the subject-matter of the land mark decisions of the Hon'ble Supreme Court. The question of construction of a Dam on Narmada River (Sardar Sarovar Project) came up for hearing before the Supreme Court in *Narmada Bachao Andolan* v. *Union of India*.[2] The Majority judgment was delivered by Mr. Justice Kripal on behalf of Dr. A.S. Anand, Chief Justice of India. The Supreme Court held as under:—

1. World Conference for Social Development, Copenhagen, 1995.
2. AIR 2000 SC 3751.

"The allegation that the said project was not in the national or public interest is not correct seeing to the need of water for burgeoning population which is most critical and important. The population of India, which is now one billion, is expected to reach a figure between 1.5 billion and 1.8 billion in the year 2050, would necessitate the need of 2788 billion cubic meter of water annually in India to be above water stress zone and 1650 billion cubic metre to avoid being water scarce country."

Regarding the vital role of such dams in providing irrigation for food security, the Supreme Court held as under:—

"Dams play a vital role in providing irrigation for food security, domestic and industrial water supply, hydroelectric power and keeping flood waters back. On full development, the Narmada has a potential of irrigating over 6 million hectares of land and generating 3000 mw of power."

The Supreme Court also referred to the report of the world Bank in 1990 in the following manner:—

"The argument in favour of the Sardar Sarovar project is that the benefits are so large that they substantially outweigh the costs of the immediate human and environmental disruption. Without the dam, the long term costs for people would be much greater and lack of an income source for future generations would put increasing pressure on the environment. If the waters of the Narmada river continue to flow to the sea unused there appears to be no alternative to escalating human deprivation, particularly in the dry areas of Gujarat. The project has the potential to feed as many as 20 million people, provide domestic and industrial water for about 30 million, employ about 1 million , and provide valuable peak electric power in an area with high unmet power demand (farm pumps often get only a few hours power per day)".

Regarding the utility of dam, the Supreme Court made the following observations:—

"The dam is neither a nuclear establishment nor a polluting industry. The construction of a dam undoubtedly would result in the change of environment but it will not be correct to presume that the construction of a large dam like the Sardar Sarovar will result in ecological disaster. India has an experience of over 40 years in the construction of dams. The experience does not show that construction of a large dam is not cost effective, or leads to ecological or environmental degradation."

The Supreme Court also referred to the benefits arising out the construction of the dam in the following manner:—

> "The petitioner has not been able to point out a single instance where the construction of a Dam has, on the whole , had an adverse environmental impact. On the contrary the environment has improved. That being so there is no reason to suspect, with all the experience gained so far, that the position here will be any different and there will not be overall improvement and prosperity". It should not be forgotten that poverty is regarded as one of the causes of degradation of environment. With improved irrigation system the people will prosper. The construction of Bhakra Dam is a shining example for all to see how the backward area of erstwhile undivided Punjab have now become the granary of India with improved environment than what was there before the completion of the Bhakra Nangal project".

In a later case reported as *Godavarman Thirumulpad* v. *Union of India,*[1] Supreme Court referred to the objectives of the Forests Policy 1988 and *inter-alia* held as under:—

"(i) Maintenance of environmental stability through preservation and, where necessary, restoration of the ecological balance that has been adversely disturbed by serious depletion of the forests of the country;

(ii) Conserving the natural heritage of the country by preserving the remaining natural forest with the vast variety of flora and fauna, which represent the remarkable biological diversity and genetic resources of the country;

(iii) Checking soil erosion and denudation in the catchment areas of rivers, lakes and reservoirs in the interest of soil and water conservation, for mitigating floods and droughts and for the retardation of siltation of reservoirs,

(iv) Checking the extension of sand dunes in the desert areas of Rajasthan and along the costal tracts;

(v) Increasing substantial the forest/tree cover in the country through massive afforestation and social forestry programmes, especially on all denuded, degraded and unproductive lands;

(vi) Meeting the requirements of fuelwood, fodder, minor forest produce and small timber of the rural and tribal populations.

The principal aim of the Forest Policy must be to ensure environmental stability and maintenance of ecological balance including

1. (2006) 1 SCC 1.

atmosphere equilibrium which are vital for sustenance of all life forms, human, animal and plant. The derivation of direct economic benefit must be subordinate to this principal aim".

The scope of the Environmental Protection Act 29 of 1986 came up for consideration before the Supreme Court in case reported as *Intellectual Forum, Tirupathi* v. *State of Andhra Pradesh*,[1] the Supreme Court held as under:

> "The responsibility of the State to protect the environment is now a well accepted notion in all countries. It is this notion that in international law, gave rise to the principle of "State responsibility" for pollution emanating within one's own territories; *Corfu Channel* case. This responsibility is clearly enunciated in the United Nations Conference on the Human Environment, Stockholm 1972 (Stockholm Convention), to which India was a party. The relevant Clause of this Declaration in the present context is Paragraph 2, which states:
>
> > The natural resources of the earth, including the air, water, land, flora and fauna and especially representative samples of natural ecosystems, must be safeguarded for the benefit of present and future generations through careful planning or management, as appropriate:"

Thus, there is no doubt about the fact that there is a responsibility bestowed upon the Government to protect and preserve the tanks, which are an important part of the environment of the area.

The Supreme Court also in this land mark judgment made a reference to the Rio Declaration of Environment Development, passed during the Earth Summit of 1992 with a particular reference to principle 4 of the said declaration.

Environment—However, reference is made in a very recent judgment in three Judges Bench of the Supreme Court of India in *T.N. Godavarman Thirumulpad* v. *Union of India*.[2] The Supreme Court analyzed the scope of interference where agreements had duly been signed between the parties at a earlier point of time and whether any direction can be given in respect of their relation to mining/refinery activities, whether the court cannot issue any direction in such case, the court held as under:—

> "The Supreme Court cannot change lease/MOU/Joint venture agreements signed between the parties at the earlier point of time which have been approved by the Ministry of Mines, Government of

---

1. AIR 2006 SC 1352.
2. (2008) 9 SCC 711.

India, and other authorities. If the counter-suggestion of CEC is accepted, namely, that the mines be taken over by SPV then it would be violating the terms and conditions of the joint venture agreement dated 5-10-2004 between OMCL and VAL (now substituted by SIIL). Moreover, the joint venture agreement dated 5-10-2004 was executed because the Government of Orissa wanted its undertaking, namely, OMCL to earn revenue on its own account. Therefore, a complete change over cannot be directed. The lease by the State of Orrisa be modified to substitute SPV instead of OMCL."

Thus, it will be seen that the Rio Declaration on environmental protection, and the later affirmation thereof goes a long way in fulfilling the cherished ambitions of the mankind. The said principles are a guide and a source of beacon light for the future generation to follow.

ROLE OF LAW IN SOCIAL AND ECONOMIC DEVELOPMENT IN ASIA PACIFIC REGION*

Law has various roles, but the role of law in social and economic development, particularly in the Asia Pacific Region is, perhaps, very vital and important in the present day context. Unless and until the countries in the Asia Pacific Region develop fully in the social and economic field, the benefits of all other laws including the law relating to human rights will become illusory for the vast masses of people living in this Region. Therefore, this subject has been rightly chosen for the APLA Conference held in New Delhi in February 1992.

In the G-15 Summit Conference in Caracas, the draft communique prepared by the officials made the point that there can be no peace dividend in the world, nor the prospect of global stability, without concern being focussed on the problems of development, since four-fifths of humanity lived in the poor countries of the South. (As per News Item from Times of India November 28, 1991).

The then Prime Minister of India, Shri P.V. Narasimha Rao, in his key-note address on the subject at the G-15 Summit's first working committee session said that it was, perhaps, for the first time in the world history that a truly global and integrated world economy was emerging. He further noted that this globalisation can be fruitful only when a conscious development dimension is introduced and becomes an integral part in this process. The Prime Minister also referred to the role of the developed countries in trying to prescribe what mankind should do and where it should go. He pointed out that:

> "The new focus, he said, seemed to be almost exclusively on the ideals of democracy, human rights and rule of law. All of these were indeed cherished values and a great deal of effort had gone into these over the years. But in all this, the central concern of development should not be lost sight of."

---

* First published in *Asia Pacific Lawyers' Association (Indian Chapter), Working Papers*, p. 1.

The Prime Minister further emphasised the essential role of development insofar as the developing countries are concerned in the following manner:—

> "Without this essential element of development, any vision of the future would necessarily remain incomplete as far as the developing countries are concerned. It would also jeopardise the very values of democracy, human rights and the rule of law, which every one admittedly wants to advance and support." (As per News Item from Hindustan Times November 29, 1991)

In fact, the guiding principles for this Seminar would be the above quoted words of the Prime Minister of India.

Mr. Li Peng, the Chinese Prime Minister made a memorable visit to India and the aspect of social and economic development was high-lighted in the meeting of these two great countries of Asia.

During the course of his talks, Mr. Li Peng pointed out that China's energies were now centered around economic development. He further pointed out as under:—

> "As the old order changed, the world had become more turbulent and unstable and in these circumstances, the developing countries had come out worse than before. It was, therefore, of utmost importance for developing countries, particularly India and China, that the two largest nations, to strengthen cooperation for peace, stability and development in the region". (As per News Item from Hindustan Times dated September 16, 1991)

The Ex-Chief Justice of the Supreme Court of India, Mr. P.N. Bhagwati, in an address in Bombay emphasised what is a text-book lesson for development jurisprudence in the following words:—

> "The right to development is one of the most important basic human rights and it constitutes the culminating point of the evolution of the concept of human rights. This super right, transcending the differentiation of civil and political rights and socio-economic rights into the future dimension, has been termed as 'human right of the third generation'. It has been recognised as an individual as well as collective right".

He further pointed out as under:—

> "If the large masses of people who inhabit the developing countries of the Third World are to achieve full and equal realisation of this right to development, it is necessary that they should have effective access to—

— tangible resources to achieve their basic needs of productive and equitably paid work, sufficient nutrition, health care and hygiene, shelter, energy, resources, clean water and air;

— the necessary intangible resources, especially education and information, to enable them better to utilise resources, and to participate freely in the process of development;

— structure of production and government to assure the fair and equitable allocation of the above resources; and

— facilities and services to organise themselves to participate, monitor, evaluate and review development programmes and processes, and to hold accountable those responsible for their implementation." (As per Main Stream Volume 24 No. 28 dated 15-3-1986, which is reproduced in the Book "Social Justice Sunset or Dawn" by V.R. Krishna Iyer).

In an Article (Planned Development, Self-Reliance and equity in the South and South-East Asian Region) Mr. Mangat Ram Aggarwal pointed out as under:—

> "Virtually all the developing countries of the so-called 'third world', since the end of the Second World War and the Socialist Countries have adopted planning for achieving an optimum allocation of resources from the society welfare point of view and accelerating the process, as quickly as possible, of economic and social growth."

It will, thus, be abundantly clear that the role of law, with which the Asia Pacific Region is vitally concerned, is the one in relation to social and economic development and this role is even more important if not equally important as the basic human rights are concerned. In fact, they can be termed "as a human rights of the Third Generation" as pointed out by Hon'ble Mr. Justice Bhagwati also.

In an article on "Developing Countries Perception of Environmental Protection and Economic Development", Mr. A. Mpazi Sinjela, working with the United Nations Office of Legal Affairs pointed out even in relation to environmental issues as under:—

> "Developing countries have always considered environmental issues in the context of north-south relations and *economic development*. They have argued that pollution of the environment was caused by the industrialized north. Furthermore, it is their view that the current concerns with environmental issues have emerged from problems arising out of pollution of the environment by the industrialized countries."

"Environmental concerns have, therefore, been viewed by the developing countries, as a shift away from their economic development goals. Their preference has been to place economic development and economic growth before the preservation of the envirorment."

Reference in relation to the role of law in social and economic development may now be made with reference to the provisions of the Constitution of India. The very Preamble of the Constitution of India, *inter alia,* promises to secure to all its citizens justice, social, economic and political and equality of status and of opportunity and assuring the dignity of individual. The fundamental rights guaranteed under Part III of the Constitution of India also deserve mention. Article 19, *inter alia,* provides for protection of certain rights including the right "to form associations or unions" and to practise any profession, or to carry on any occupation, trade or business [Articles 19(c) and 19(g)]. The right to the Constitutional Remedies is provided under clause/article 32 of the Constitution to move the Supreme Court for enforcement of rights conferred by Part III of the Constitution. Reference may also be made to certain principles of Policy to be followed by the State mentioned in Part IV, dealing with Directive Principles of State Policy.

Article 39 of the Constitution of India reads as under:—

"39. Certain principles of policy to be followed by the State. The State shall, in particular, direct its policy towards securing—

(a) that the citizens, men and women, equally have the right to an adequate means to livelihood;

(b) that the ownership and control of the material resources of the community are so distributed as best to subserve the common good;

(c) that the operation of the economic system does not result in the concentration of wealth and means of production to the common detriment;

(d) that there is equal pay for equal work for both men and women;

(e) that the health and strength of workers, men and women, and the tender age of the children are not abused and the citizens are not forced by economic necessity to enter avocations unsuited to their age or strength;

(f) that children are given opportunities and facilities to develop in a healthy manner and in conditions of freedom and dignity and that childhood and youth are protected against exploitation and against moral and material abandonment."

It will, thus, be abundantly clear that the social and economic developments are given a prime importance, in the role of law, inasmuch as they have been given a prominent position in the Constitution of India itself. The Municipal laws of this country also take into account the social and economic development aspects and it is the earnest hope of the author that the present article will also give inspiration to the other countries in the Asia Pacific Region, to take the lead and be pioneers in giving the role of law a prominent place in social and economic development of their respective regions.

TERRORISM AND THE HUMAN RIGHTS

The scope of the Human Rights is indeed a panoramic one and stands widely expanded. It does not only cover the basic civil and political rights but also a wide range of new rights which are socio-economic and other rights, which are necessary for the enjoyment of the Human Rights.

For the protection of human rights, reference may be made to the National Human Rights Commission, which has been created under the Act of Parliament to see that human rights are fully protected. The Human Rights Commission has a unique role in creating an awareness of the human rights and also issuing necessary directions of human rights.

However, recent instances of terrorism have shaken the very fabric, not only of Indian Society but the entire world. The instances of terrorism are on the rise in the whole world and recent instance of the same include attack on Indian Parliament on 13th December, 2001, attack on Jammu & Kashmir Assembly on 1st October, 2001, attack on Akshardham Temple on 24th September, 2002, attack on U.S. Information Center at Kolkatta on 22nd January, 2002, Srinagar CRPF Camp attack on 22nd November, 2002, IED blast near Jawahar Tunnel on 23rd Novemebr, 2002, attack on Raghunath Mandir on 24th November, 2002, Bus stand blast at Ghatkopar in Mumbai on 2nd December, 2002, attack on villagers in Nadimarg in Pulwama District in Jammu & Kashmir on the night of 23rd - 24th March, 2003, etc.

As pointed out in *Peoples Union for Civil Liberties* v. *Union of India*,[1] "terrorists acts are meant to destabilize the nation by challenging its sovereignty and integrity to raze Constitutional principles that we hold dear, to create a psyche of fear and anarchism among common people, to tear apart the secular fabric, to overthrow democratically elected government, to promote prejudice and bigotry, to demoralize the security forces, to thwart the economic progress and development and so on. This cannot be equated with a usual law and order problem within a State. On the other hand, it is inter-State, international or cross-border in character.

1. AIR 2004 SC 456.

Fight against the overt and covert acts of terrorism is not a regular criminal justice endeavour. Rather it is defence of our nation and its citizens. It is a challenge to the whole nation and invisible force of Indianness that binds this great nation together. Therefore, terrorism is a new challenge for law enforcement. By indulging in terrorist activities organized groups or individuals, trained, inspired and supported by fundamentalists and anti-Indian elements were trying to destabilize the country. This new breed of menace was hitherto unheard of. Terrorism is definitely a criminal act, but it is much more than mere criminality. Today, the government is charged with the duty of protecting the unity, integrity, secularism and sovereignty of India from terrorists both from outside and within borders. To face terrorism we need new approaches, techniques, weapons, expertise and of course new laws."

"The terrorist threat we are facing is now on an unprecedented global scale. Terrorism has been a global threat with global effects. It has become a challenge to the whole community of civilized nations. Terrorist activities in one country may take on a transnational character, carrying out attacks across one border, receiving funding from private parties or a government across another and procuring arms from multiple sources. Terrorism in a single country can readily become a threat to regional peace and security owing to its spillover effects. It is, therefore, difficult in the present context to draw sharp distinctions between domestic and international terrorism".

"The Security Council unanimously passed resolutions 1368(2001) and 1373(2001); the General Assembly adopted resolutions 56/1 by consensus, and convened a special session. All these resolutions and declarations *inter alia* call upon member States to take necessary steps to 'prevent and suppress terrorist acts' and also to 'prevent and suppress the financing of terrorist acts'. India is a party to all these resolves. Anti-terrorism activities in the global level are mainly carried out through bilateral and multilateral co-operation among nations. It has, thus, become our international obligation also to pass necessary laws to fight terrorism".

"The important question, therefore, arises as to what is the role of human rights *qua* acts of terrorism. The role has been thus clarified by the Supreme Court "the protection and promotion of human rights under the rule of law is essential in the prevention of terrorism. Here comes the role of law and court's responsibility. If human rights are violated in the process of combating terrorism, it will be self-defeating. Terrorism often thrives where human rights are violated, which adds to the need to strengthen action to combat violations of human rights. The lack of hope for justice provides breeding grounds for terrorism. Terrorism itself should also be understood as an assault on basic rights. In all cases, the fight against terrorism must be respectful to the human rights. Our Constitution lays down clear limitations on the State actions within the context of the fight against terrorism".

Mr. Justice S.B. Sinha, Retired Judge Supreme Court of India in his article "Human Rights and Judiciary" published in the Human Rights Year Book 2008 has dealt with the terrorism in the following manner:—

> "Perhaps the most heated debates concerning the protection of human rights in the criminal justice delivery system have occurred with respect to terrorism that poses a clear and present danger to the sovereignty and integrity of our Nation. The now repealed Protection of Terrorism Act, 2002 had created much controversy when it sought to incorporate "special measures" into the ordinary criminal justice system. For instance, POTA allowed for extended police custody, intrusive police investigation, admission of police confessions in trial, and summary procedures in special courts. Such deliberations on the balance required between the protection of human rights on the one hand, and the interests of national security on the other, are however, not specific to India alone. The rise of fundamentalism and international terrorist organisations has made countries around the world gravitated in favour of more stringent measures for the safety of their people. Needless to say, in many cases an Guantanamo Bay is only one example—the necessities of national security have resulted in large-scale violations of human rights."

In this connection he has quoted various judgments as follows:

> *Abhasi* v. *Secretary of State for Foreign and Commonwealth Affairs*[1]—the courts of Appeal (Queen's Bench);
>
> *Rasul et al.* v. *Bush, President of the United States;*[2]
>
> *Hamidi et al.* v. *Rumsfeld, Secretary of Defence;*[3] and
>
> *Rumsfeld* v. *Pudilla.*[4]

The learned Judged has further pointed as under:—

> "This 'balancing of interests' between the rights of the detainees and the interest of national security is an essential characteristic of a fair trial".

---

1. 2002 EWCA Civ 1598 (QB).
2. (2004) 72 USLW 4596.
3. (2004) 72 USLW 4607.
4. (2004) 72 USLW 4594.

Mr. Justice Altamas Kabir, Judge Supreme Court of India and Vice-President, International Institute of Human Rights Society in his article published in the Human Rights Year Book 2009 has dealt with the terrorism in the following manner:—

> "One of the more recent and dangerous trends is terrorism and its politicization for political ends. It is often said that all is fair in love and war and politics is certainly a war for power, but certainly not at the cost of the nation. Instead of working in unison to combat this heinous evil and crime against humanity, acts of terrorism are used with impugnity to create vote banks, which is, in fact, destroying the very soul of the Constitution, which, one can say without fear of contradiction, is the finest written Constitution in the worlds, and is creating hate banks instead.

He has further stated in his article "Basic Fundamental Rights" and the Indian Response in the following manner:—

> "it would like take hours to cover even a minuscule portion of the worldwide transgressions of Human and Fundamental Rights and the right to live a life of human dignity, but it is heartening and reassuring that attempts are at least being made by the world community to contain the poison that has permeated society throughout the world. In India, courts, and in particular the High Courts and the Supreme Court, have always been the guardian of Human Rights and liberties of its citizens, and have within their jurisdiction come down heavily on their transgressions either by the police, the executive or even by the legislature while enacting laws, which seek to curtail such rights and liberties. In other words, the courts have always striven to uphold the Rule of Law and to protect and preserve the basic and fundamental rights guaranteed to the citizens of this country, most of which are Human Rights contained either in Part II of the Constitution or in Part IV. Even as recently as in 2007, a Nine-Judge Bench of the Supreme Court, while considering the case of *I.R. Coelho* v. *State of Tamil Nadu,*[1] unanimously reiterated and affirmed that the basic structure of the Constitution, which also includes the Human and Fundamental Rights contained in Parts III and IV of the Constitution, could not be altered. We can only hope that the future holds a better deal for those who inherit it".

---

1. (2007) 2 SCC 1.

It will thus be seen that terrorism is condemned universally and, it is being realised that terrorism is an assault on human rights and it is terrorism which is cutting at the roots of the human rights of peace loving people all over the world.

PART V

IN THE SPIRIT OF LETTERS*

* Author's Letters to the Editor published in several newspapers

IN THE SPIRIT OF LETTERS

UGLY STATUES*

Sir,—Mr. Nehru recently condemned the production and sale of crude and ugly statues and paintings of national leaders, particularly Mahatma Gandhi. As a lover of art, probably it has hurt him to see inartistic paintings and statues of national leaders.

But one of the reasons for this seems to be the respect and liking which the common people have towards their leaders. Even the poorest of the poor do like to exhibit in their homes paintings and statues of national leaders. They do not mind if they are inartistic. A ready market is, therefore, assured for all such cheap and inartistic paintings.

The remedy lies in production of simple and plain statues and photos of our national leaders which even an average Indian may be able to purchase.

Yours
Keshav Dayal

* Appeared in *The Hindustan Times* on August 31, 1954.

LANGUAGE PROBLEM*

Sir,—Language is one of the most vital and fundamental part of a people's way of living and thinking. Every language has a literature, culture and traditions of its own which sustain the people by whom it is spoken. There is at present a great controversy regarding the role of regional languages as against role of the national language. Frustration and resentment, seem to prevail among a large section of the people. There can, however, be no two opinions regarding the importance of Hindi as the official language of the country. But why should there be ill feeling regarding the development of other regional languages? All languages are equally sacred, and their development should be our common aim. Opening up of a separate regional language institute in every university in the country would go a long way to fulfil this aim. These institutes should have proper personnel, and take up the study of various regional languages in right earnest. These institutes should also organise, cultural, educational and social functions of the various regions to give a complete background of the languages. They will also help greatly in realizing the cultural unity of the nation.

To encourage these institutes, it should be made compulsory for everyone to learn at least one regional language before getting the university degree. Private institutions, clubs and societies should also take interest in the matter.

Yours
Keshav Dayal

---

* Appeared in *The Hindustan Times* on February 20, 1956.

PREVENTIVE DETENTION*

Sir,—I have read with interest your editorial on preventive detention. Civil liberty is no doubt the most cherished of ideals. Curtailment of civil liberties can have little justification in peace time. However, it is pertinent to ask whether conditions in the country have considerably improved to warrant the abolition of the Preventive Detention Act. The recent disturbances in Bombay, Calcutta and other places prove they have not. The country is on the threshold of the second Five-Year Plan, and we cannot hope to fight the evils of unemployment and low income in the midst of violent and illegal strikes. In the circumstances the Government are fully justified in extending the measure till at least the reorganization of States has been effected.

Yours

Keshav Dayal

---

* Appeared in *The Hindustan Times* on June 10, 1956.

HONESTY THE BEST POLICY*

Sir,—The question of honesty can be discussed in theoretical as well as practical terms. Theoretically speaking, honesty is of the greatest value for our moral and spiritual development. It is to be practiced for the attainment of a higher and nobler life. Our civilisation, in the ultimate analysis, is to be judged by the development of such values as honesty, truth and beauty. In India, since time immemorial, very great stress has been laid on leading an honest and pure life. In theory, therefore, I entirely agree with the views expressed by Dr. Mulk Raj Anand and put honesty on a pedestal.

However, evaluated from a practical point of view, honest people invariably suffer innumerable hardships in this corrupt, materialistic world. In everyday life, we find honest, sincere and truthful people being slowly crushed, under the wheels of tyranny and oppression. It is difficult for a man honest as daylight to make friends and live at peace with the world. He tends to become a lonely, isolated individual, chasing ideals. We do come across some very honest people who have succeeded in life. However, a closer examination would reveal that other factors, such as personal ability, capacity for work, family connections, academic and other qualifications are responsible for their success in life.

Weighing the *pros and cons* of the matter carefully, I think it is wrong to uphold honesty as the best policy.

Yours
Keshav Dayal

---

* Appeared in *The Illustrated Weekly of India* on August 19, 1956.

SHOULD MERCY-KILLING BE ALLOWED?*

Sir—Dr. Parmar has condemned the idea of mercy-killing on two counts. The first of these is that, since man cannot create, he has no right to destroy. The second is that, since man is not infallible in his prognostications regarding the future of a patient, it is assuming too great a responsibility to relieve the agony of the victim.

According to the first notion, man should not interfere in matters relating to birth and death, which are a divine prerogative. Accordingly, birth control will be ruled out. While believing in the all-pervading, omnipotent and omniscient power of God, I do not subscribe to the above view. God has given man liberty to shape his destiny. All the great men of the world have emphasised that reason and not blind faith or dogmas should guide our actions. Therefore, if on humanitarian grounds it is felt that a man is prey to unlimited suffering, with death only a matter of time, his living is a greater torture than even death.

The second proposition is not at all controversial. If there is even a semblance of hope of recovery from unbearable suffering and pain, there can be no reason for mercy-killing.

Yours

Keshav Dayal

---

* Appeared in *The Illustrated Weekly of India* on February 17, 1957.

LAW'S DELAYS*

Sir—I entirely agree with the views expressed in your editorial 'Law's Delays' that the case for speeding up the administration of justice cannot be left pending for long. Delay in the conclusion of cases is becoming frequent and seems to be on the increase. Most of the land and immovable property cases take years for disposal in the normal course. It is not uncommon to find litigation being continued from father to son and even grandsons. One of the reasons for delay in the disposal of cases is the seeking of unnecessary adjournments by the litigants. You have rightly pointed out that applications for adjournments should be carefully looked into. Of course in some cases the granting of adjournment may be necessary and even essential for serving the ends of justice. Another reason for delay is the paucity of judges. In some States the number of pending cases has reached a frightening figure, and the only solution lies in the appointment of additional members of the Bench. But the important reason, in my view, is inherent in law and cannot be easily solved. The Civil Procedure Code provides in the normal course the right of two appeals. In cases where a second appeal is not provided for, there is the right of revision to High Court in some cases. Most of the cases are conducted first in the lower courts, then in appellate courts and then in High Court. This necessarily involves delay. But the right of appeal is a sacred one and cannot be scoffed at. However, delays can only be avoided by bringing in more efficiency in the administration of justice.

Yours
Keshav Dayal

* Appeared in *The Hindustan Times* on June 26, 1957.

LAW'S DELAYS*

Sir,—The appointment of a four-man committee to go into the causes of delay in the disposal of cases in civil courts is a step in the right direction. The committee will be able to tackle the problem of law's delay from a practical point of view. It is gratifying to know that the authorities, which are dealing with the problems, are those really connected with the work of administration or law. The other step, namely, the treatment of all appeals in which stay orders have been issued on an urgent basis, is also a step in the right direction. The engagement of juniors in all important cases, would not only help in expediting cases, but would also help the juniors in passing through a critical time of their life. In addition it will give them the benefit of working and learning with those who have reached the ladder of success in the profession. Another way which can greatly help in disposal of the cases is closer scrutiny in the prayers for adjournments. However, sometimes interests of justice require that an adjournment should be granted. The judge should, therefore, keep in mind that adjournments should only be granted in fit and proper cases, and not as a matter of course. Cases which are old, or in which the record is lengthy and they are expected to take a long time, should be given priority. Very old cases may be taken from day to day, or week to week, as far as possible. The problem of delay in the disposal of cases can only be tackled with the co-operation of the members of the Bar and the Bench. They should join hands to restore the confidence of the people in the administration of Justice.

Yours

Keshav Dayal

---

* Appeared in *The Hindustan Times* on January 25, 1958.

LAW RESEARCH*

Sir,—The Chief Justice of India, Mr. B.P. Sinha, inaugurating the All-India Law Conference at Patna recently, has rightly emphasized the importance of research in law in a co-ordinated and integrated way. The country has aimed at the establishment of a welfare State, and it is necessary for this purpose that our laws should keep pace with the fast-changing society. Law has to be adopted to these changing conditions of society, and it is here that there is great scope for research in law. Unfortunately, however there is at present no incentive for those seeking to do legal research. Research can only be carried out in an atmosphere and environment of social and economic security. Are we offering these to those who are prepared to do research in law? And are there enough avenues for the law aspirants to take to research as a profession?

Young law graduates and junior members of the Bar should be offered greater avenues and opportunities for research in law. They should be provided with social and economic security which is a prerequisite of research work.

Yours

Keshav Dayal

* Appeared in *The Hindustan Times* on April 22, 1960.

INDIAN MUSLIMS*

Sir,—I was surprised to read the speech of Maulana Fakhruddin at the recent annual session of the Jamiat-ul-Ulema-I-Hind at Ujjain. He is reported to have said: "The secular character of the Indian Constitution is a challenge to every community to look after its cultural and religious traditions at its own expense, if they were not to suffer an eclipse and eventual extinction." He has accused the authorities of treating the Muslims as if they had no equal status with their majority brethren and has urged the Union Government to appoint a commission to inquire into the treatment meted out to the Muslims.

The whole speech smacks of a fanatical religious fervour which is aimed at playing with the sentiments, emotions and passions of the Muslims and reminds one of the role of the Muslim League. The Constitution declares in unequivocal terms about equal treatment to be given to the people irrespective of caste, religion or culture. It guarantees that there shall be no interference in the religious belief, education, and culture of any community.

If the charge against the Constitution is that it does not help the cause of religion, then the same is not peculiar to the Muslims alone. Furthermore, the difficulties, both internal and external, which the country is facing today are not peculiar to any particular community and can only be tackled on a national scale.

Yours
Keshav Dayal

* Appeared in *The Hindustan Times* on December 17, 1960.

HIGH COURT DELAYS*

Sir,—I admit that to a certain extent delay in disposal of cases is due to an increase of cases in which the State is a party. No doubt litigation between the public and the State has increased beyond all proportions. There are so many bodies and organisations which are either Government aided or under direct Government control, and this has resulted in an increase of litigation. The setting up of a Government agency to investigate cases in which the State is likely to be a party before they actually come to the court would be a step in the right direction, as suggested by Mrs. R.K. Gupta. I do not think awarding of exemplary costs against the State to be recovered from erring officers would be in keeping with good traditions, as suggested by Mr. H.C. Mittal.

However, to say that delay in disposal of cases is only because of increasing litigation, in which the State is a party, is to look at the matter from a lop-sided view. One of the main reasons for delays is the paucity of judges. Appointment of additional members of the Bench would go a long way in disposing of pending cases. Sometimes vacancies are not filled for months together.

Another reason for delay is the non-availability of senior counsel because of heavy work. Engagement of juniors in all cases would help in expediting cases. Old cases and cases in which proceedings of the trial courts have been stayed should be given top priority. The co-operation of the members of the Bar and the Bench is also important. They should join hands to restore public confidence in the administration of justice.

Yours
Keshav Dayal

---

* Appeared in *The Hindustan Times* on August 21, 1961.

TASKS BEFORE JUDICIARY*

Sir,—This is with reference to the article by the Chief Justice Sabyasachi Mukharji on the subject of legal system, "Problems and Challenges" (HT, April 30). The Chief Justice has taken pains in detailing the various recommendations of the Law Commission and analysing the problems and challenges being faced by the legal system all over the country. A detailed analysis has been made which should be instructive to all those connected with the Bar and the Judiciary. It has been rightly pointed out that the obvious remedy which has been repeatedly recommended but not acted upon in right earnest in cutting down delay is the appointment of judges of unimpeachable integrity to the superior courts and increasing their strength on a realistic assessment of workload. The question arises as to why constitutional functionaries are not able to find men of integrity and proven merits. The blame has to be shared by all involved in appointing judges to the High Courts and the Supreme Court.

There can be no doubt that an apolitical, efficient, dedicated, honest and upright judiciary is the prime requisite and it must be fearless, if the rule of law has any meaning in this country.

Some of the other suggestions made in the article relate to the functioning of the Chief Justice of the High Court who has to take special care in the formulation of Benches and the appointment of specialised judges for specific fields of law.

It has been rightly pointed out that the judiciary has remained outside the mainstream of technological advancement and the suggestion made in this behalf should be implemented by the Supreme Court itself and by the various High Courts in this country.

The article on the whole should prove stimulating to the members of the Bar and the Bench and all other interested in the welfare of the country. It is hoped that the concerned constitutional authorities would take due note of the suggestions made and, in any case, there would be no delay in the appointment of men of integrity and proven merits for the higher courts. It is expected that political and other such considerations will not influence the appointment of judges in the Supreme Court and High Courts.

Yours

Keshav Dayal

---

* Appeared in *The Hindustan Times* on May 5, 1990.

DEFECTION*

Sir,—I have read the opinion of the eminent constitutional expert Dr. L.M. Singhvi upholding the constitutional validity of a breakaway group of the Janata Dal forming the Janata Dal-S as its strength was more than 1/3 of the undivided Janata Dal in the Lok Sabha (HT, Nov. 17). His views appear to be sound and in consonance with the provision of the 10th Schedule of the Constitution which is inserted by the Constitution (52nd Amendment) Act of 1985.

I have also seen the article of Mr. M.C. Bhandare, "Disqualification: Make it Justiciable" (HT, Nov. 19), wherein he has suggested that the question of disqualification should be made a justiciable issue.

The views of the learned MP require to be fully examined by constitutional experts, as the questions raised are of far-reaching importance to Parliamentary democracy.

Yours
Keshav Dayal

---

* Appeared in *The Hindustan Times* on December 19, 1990.

MONSTROUS TAXATION*

Sir,—I have read N.A. Palkhivala's article "A monstrous tax structure" (HT, Oct. 30). The writer is not only an eminent constitutional expert, but is also an authority on tax laws and economic matters connected therewith. He has rightly pointed out, "The most persistent tendency in India has been to have too much government and too little administration; too many laws and too little justice; too many public servants and too little public service; too many controls and too little welfare. Every segment of the people's enterprise is festooned with red tape,"

It is high time that those in power try to take the bull by the horns and take the necessary drastic steps which can revitalise the economic situation. I join the writer in hoping that the country will be able to find a leader who can light the imagination of the entire nation, at this critical juncture.

Yours
Keshav Dayal

* Appeared in *The Hindustan Times* on November 11, 1991.

JUDGES CAN BE PROSECUTED*

Sir,—Re the news item "Judges can be prosecuted: SC" (HT, July 26). In a historic judgment in the case of a former Chief Justice of the Madras High Court *K. Veeraswami* v. *Union of India*, (1991) 3 SCC 655 the Supreme Court has held that the Prevention of Corruption Act applies to judges of the High Court and the highest court majority of 4:1.

The decision is historic for it is the first time that the President will be bound by the advice of the Chief Justice of India instead of by the Council of Ministers. The judges were, however, not unanimous on how it should be implemented and as rightly pointed out in your editorial (HT July 27) the gap between the procedure and process for dealing with allegations of impropriety and misconduct remain as wide as ever.

Yours
Keshav Dayal

---

* Appeared in *The Hindustan Times* on September 16, 1991.

Part VI

Poetically Yours

POETICALLY YOURS

GOLDEN WEDDING ANNIVERSARY

This Anniversary is special, it is Gold
May the same usher in happiness untold
And bring in all-round prosperity in its fold
This Golden Anniversary Function
Let every one present behold.

Son, Daughter and Grandsons follow the mould
To celebrate the occasion Money consideration
shouldn't hold,
Love and Respect to parents is not to be told
To Wine and Dine, We are never old.

Fifty years of living together
Through a tough and rough weather
Enough to provide peace of mind
And pleasures of a different kind

This Anniversary is special, it is Gold
May the same usher in happiness untold.

LYING ON GRASS

1. While lying on the cool green grass
   All my troubles seem to pass,
   The wheel of time passes by
   While in the cool shadows I lie
2. With fresh and new ideas I, think
   All my sorrows seem to sink
   I see a world of myriad light
   Dancing figures in extreme delight
3. When I glance at the row of flowers
   I forget all, I look on for hours
   The green grass on me a spell does cast
   Joy and happiness for long they last.

TEMPTATION

Oh temptation,
Before thy temple
Even the sages often bowed-
Upright Moralists,
Religious Teachers, Socialists,
Idealists and their like
Victory over Temptation
Nature never allowed!
Men often seem to guess –
temptation we have conquered
Oh how they are mistaken
their temptation must be less!

FREEDOM

Man's great desire
For eternal Freedom
can he even achieve?
Every moment of life
that man leads,
knowest not he, life depends
on the air, that he breaths.
The doctrine of freedom
that is proclaimed –
How long can it deceive?
Is freedom possible?
Man's greatest passion –
Is'nt it a wild dream, a great delusion?
The charm of life, like a hunter's net.
Has caught man in its meshes –
For man to live in peace
from birth to doomsday,
compromise of Freedom
Is the price man has to pay.

EGOISM

The world has witnessed
Men, strong, bold and true –
Inspired with faith and courage
Great heights they achieved
Name and fame to them accrue –
But the work most sublime
Man can ever do –
Being no exceptions
Are tainted with egoism too
Saints, reformers and the sages
great works have they done
So their name may be cherished
Their contemporary should be none.
Is egoism the impulse
The driving force of all
That is done –
Or is it an enemy unknown
victory over which
Man has never won?

DRIVING A CAR

1. When I have to go far
   I do not travel by car,
   there is nothing much wrong,
   Only it takes a bit long

2. To drive the car when I sit,
   I seem to lose all my wit,
   Accelerator how much to press,
   Always puts me in distress.

3. When I have to change the gear,
   I try to remove all my fear,
   But I fail to press the clutch,
   and the car gets a jerky touch.

4. When I reach the crossing range;
   the light signals seem to change,
   I make my grip on the wheel tight,
   To apply the brakes with full might.

5. When I see lovely faces pass,
   Yonder walking on the grass;
   I wish to see how they tread,
   But how can I control the speed.

6. When driving the car after dark;
   it is a problem how to park;
   there are vehicles on both your sides,
   and risk to your own car besides.

7. All night, while driving take my tip,
   Do not forget to make your lights dip,
   Otherwise you might get a white glare,
   Along with a threatening stare.
   Do you want to become a Jonte fan
   then travel always by "Pull Man".

OLD AGE

Limbs weaken, energy fades
Through darkness man wades;
when all efforts seem to fail,
In desperation man doth wail.

Face wrinkled, eyes dim
expression gloomy, body thin,
Muscles one of strength and might
In old age present a pitiable sight,

Like a beast on its prey,
How death holds man at bay,
Name and fame of what avail,
In the end death will prevail.

LIFE

1. Life to me a riddle poses –
Why thorns abound
Round the Dainty beds of roses,
When all seems lost –
Hope and faith are shattered
Why help comes from quarters
Unknown and never thought of?
The lesson of morality
not from the sermons reach –
It's the Drunkards
Lesson of Temperance, they truly teach

2. Man lives happy and gay –
When misery and frustration engulf
Can he ever find the way?
Men who stand erect
By honesty make their way
Why do trifles at Times
Make them sway?
Thousands lay down their life,
While a few achieve glory,
Its most unjust,
But nature repeats the story.

CLINTON'S VISIT

Is Clinton's visit a mere matter of fate?
Is the purpose—Indo-U.S. relations update?
Clinton's visit is it like that of Bill Gate?
Will it open up dollars flood gate?
Poor peoples burden will it alleviate?
Tension between India and Pakistan will it escalate?
Will chances of war in the sub-continent abate?
Or is U.S.A. arrogating to it power to subjudicate
Or mere friendship with India—it will reiterate
For after effects of Clinton's visit—one has to wait.

INDIA'S NUCLEAR TEST

Day of Pokhran Blast, what a day!
National Pride had its sway
Danger signals on the way
But come whatever may.
Indians call it a glorious day
People all over the country pray
Indians' power, has come to stay
whatever the P-5 Nations may say
Nation's future only herein lay.
Will the blast lead to arms race?
Will Nuclear Powers, India face?
Will India be forced to retrace
or towards Armaments, reduce its pace?
The country has acted with grace
In world community, India will find a place.

LAW'S DELAYS

It is the story of Laws delay
Young men files a civil suit
Only grandsons are alive and present
To appear on the Judgment day

It's lawyers only who make hay
Litigants have a real bad day,
Can the sufferers, hope for a ray?
For sure I cannot possibly say.

Law's delay, can't Judges find a way
If they try real hard
And put their learning to full play
In quest of justice, they may.

MAURITIUS VISIT

In Mauritius we met Sarah the guide
who took us round for a ride.
She came rushing like a tide
in a moment she was sitting by my side.
She planted on my cheek a big kiss
Did my heart beat a miss.
Oh what a beautiful ride
I have nothing more to hide

Author with Justice A. M. Ahmadi, former Chief Justice of India

Seated with Author, Vice President, Executive Committee, Delhi High Court Bar Association
P.L. Vohra, President, Delhi High Court Bar Association
Y.K. Sabharwal, then Hon. Secretary, Delhi High Court Bar Association, former Chief Justice of India
and B.N. Kirpal, former Chief Justice of India

Author with Justice Nasim Hasan Shah, former Chief Justice of Pakistan and Justice Sanjay Kishan Kaul, Judge, Delhi High Court

Author with Justice Nasim Hasan Shah, former Chief Justice of Pakistan and others

Author with K.K. Venugopal, Harbhagwan Singh, Justice U.C. Banerjee, Abhishek Singhvi, Former A.S.G. , Mrs. Jayshree Anand, Justice B.A. Khan and others

Author with (L–R) Rakesh Munjal, Justice B.A. Khan, Jayashree Anand, Abhishek Singhvi, K.K. Venugopal, Justice U.C. Banjejee, Mr. Harbhagwan Singh, Sudhir Gupta, Hemant Batra, A.K. Ganguly and others

(Left to Right) Author with Dr. Manish Arora (Director of Universal Law Publishing Co. Pvt. Ltd.), Hon'ble The Chief Justice Mr. A.P. Shah (Retd.) Delhi High Court, Hon'ble Member of Parliament & Senior Advocate Shri Abhishek Manu Singhvi, at the launch of the book "Famous Lawyers of Freedom Struggle and Trials of Freedom Fighters".

Author with K.K. Venugopal, Harbhagwan Singh, Justice U.C. Banerjee, Abhishek Singhvi, Former A.S.G. , Mrs. Jayshree Anand, Justice B.A. Khan and others

Author with (L–R) Rakesh Munjal, Justice B.A. Khan, Jayashrec Anand, Abhishek Singhvi, K.K. Venugopal, Justice U.C. Banjejee, Mr. Harbhagwan Singh, Sudhir Gupta, Hemant Batra, A.K. Ganguly and others

(L–R) Shradul Shroff, Abhishek Singhvi, Justice J.S. Verma, M.C. Bhandare and Mr. Keshav Dayal

Author speaking at the 8th SAARCLAW Conference

SAARCLAW Meeting

Author receiving Prize from
D. Falshaw, Chief Justice,
Punjab High Court

Author on his appointment
as President, Lions Club,
Delhi Central/Delhi South.
Justice Inder Dua, Judge,
Delhi High Court, speaking

Mr. and Mrs. Bishambar Dayal, parents

Author with wife

(Standing) Deepak Dayal, son; Sanjay Prasad, son-in-law
(L-R) Nutan, Daughter-in-law, author with wife and daughter, Alka

Author and wife with son, Deepak and daughter-in-law, Nutan

Alka's son and daughter, Ashish and Aditi; and
Deepak's children, Mrinalini and Himanshu (sitting lower)

Author performing Magic and Cards Tricks

(Left to Right) Shri S. Shroff, Adv., Hon'ble Chief Justice of India, Mr. J.S. Verma (Retd.), Shri M.C. Bhandare, Hon'ble Governor of Orissa & Author at SAARC LAW - India Chapter

(Left to Right) Author with Dr. Manish Arora (Director of Universal Law Publishing Co. Pvt. Ltd.), Hon'ble The Chief Justice Mr. A.P. Shah (Retd.) Delhi High Court, Hon'ble Member of Parliament & Senior Advocate Shri Abhishek Manu Singhvi, at the launch of the book "Famous Lawyers of Freedom Struggle and Trials of Freedom Fighters".

(Left to Right) Hon'ble Mr. Justice Sanjay Kishan Kaul, Hon'ble Mr. Justice A.K. Sikri of Delhi High Court and Ex-Member (Lady) Smt. Rajyalaxmi Rao, NCDRC, New Delhi and many others present at the launch of the book "Famous Lawyers of Freedom Struggle and Trials of Freedom Fighters".

(Left to Right) Shri Prahlad Dayal, Adv. (Author's brother), Author (in the Middle) and on extreme Right Mr. Deepak Dayal, Adv. (Author's Son) along with other dignitaries at the launch of the book "Famous Lawyers of Freedom Struggle and Trials of Freedom Fighters".

(Left to Right) Smt. Roop Dayal (Author's Wife) and Author presenting the book "Famous Lawyers of Freedom Struggle and Trials of Freedom Fighters" to Dr. Hamid Ansari, Hon'ble Vice President of India

Author presenting the book "Famous Lawyers of Freedom Struggle and Trials of Freedom Fighters" to Shri M.C. Bhandare, Hon'ble Governor of Orissa.

Author presenting the book "Famous Lawyers of Freedom Struggle and Trials of Freedom Fighters" to Hon'ble Dr. A.P.J. Abdul Kalam, Former President of India.

Author presenting the book "Famous Lawyers of Freedom Struggle and Trials of Freedom Fighters" to Shri P. Chidambaram, Hon'ble Union Home Minister.

Author presenting the book "Famous Lawyers of Freedom Struggle and Trials of Freedom Fighters" to Shri Kapil Sibal, Hon'ble Union Minister of Human Resource Development.

Author & Author's wife presenting the book "Famous Lawyers of Freedom Struggle and Trials of Freedom Fighters" to Shri Pawan Kumar Bansal, Hon'ble Union Minister of Parliamentary Affairs & Water Resources.

Author (along with other personalities) presenting the book "Famous Lawyers of Freedom Struggle and Trials of Freedom Fighters" to Shri Tejendra Khanna, Hon'ble Lt. Governor of Delhi.

Author presenting the book "Famous Lawyers of Freedom Struggle and Trials of Freedom Fighters" to Smt. Shiela Dixit, Hon'ble Chief Minister of NCT of Delhi.